Architectural Design

Food + The City

Guest-edited by Karen A Franck

 WILEY-ACADEMY

Architectural Design

Vol 75 No 3 May/June 2005

Editorial Offices
International House
Ealing Broadway Centre
London W5 5DB
T: +44 (0)20 8326 3800
F: +44 (0)20 8326 3801
E: architecturaldesign@wiley.co.uk

Editor
Helen Castle

Editorial and Design Management
Mariangela Palazzi-Williams

Art Direction/Design
Christian Küsters (CHK Design)

Design Assistant
Hannah Dumphy (CHK Design)

**Project Coordinator
and Picture Editor**
Caroline Ellerby

Advertisement Sales
Faith Pidduck/Wayne Frost
01243 770254
fpidduck@wiley.co.uk

Editorial Board
Will Alsop, Denise Bratton, Adriaan
Beukers, André Chaszar, Peter Cook,
Teddy Cruz, Max Fordham, Massimiliano
Fuksas, Edwin Heathcote, Anthony Hunt,
Charles Jencks, Jan Kaplicky, Robert
Maxwell, Jayne Merkel, Monica Pidgeon,
Antoine Predock, Michael Rotondi, Leon
van Schaik, Ken Yeang

Contributing Editors
André Chaszar
Craig Kellogg
Jeremy Melvin
Jayne Merkel

ISBN-10 0470093285
ISBN-13 9780470093283
Profile No 175

Abbreviated positions:
b=bottom, c=centre, l=left, r=right

Front and back cover: Vegetables by Turnips at
Borough Market, London.
Photo © Helen Peyton.

AD
p 4 © Helen Peyton; pp 5-7, 8(tr & b) & 10 ©
Karen A Franck; p 8 (tl) © Karen A Franck, photo
Ruth Rae; p 9 courtesy Camargue PR, © Sallie
Magnante; pp 11-14, 15(b) & 17-19 © Rachel
Hurst; pp 15(t) & 16 © Claudio Benassi; pp 20-5
© Nisha A Fernando; pp 26 & 30-4 courtesy
Toshin-Kaihatsu; p 28 © Brizhead Inc, photos
Ayako Mizuno; pp 35, 39(b), 41(r) & 42 © Project
for Public Spaces; p 36 © Hugh A Boyd
Architects; p 37(b) Alessandro DeGregori; p 37(t)
© Scott Braley; pp 38 & 39(t) © Karen A Franck;
p 40 © Anthony F Holmes; p 41(l) © Miles Wolf;
pp 43-5, 47 & 48(b) © Danai Thaitakoo; pp 46,
48(t), 49(t) & 50-1 © Brian McGrath; p 52 ©
Federico Grazzini & Gil Doron; pp 53 & 56 © Gil
Doron; p 55(t) © Bohn & Viljoen Architects; p
55(b) © John Puttick; p 57 © Columbia
University in the City of New York; p 58(t) ©
MVRDV; p 58(b) © ADAGP, Paris and DACS, London
2005; p 59 © Justin Bridgland, Mark Taylor and
Andrew Wood; pp 60 & 62-3 © Katherine KY Ng;
pp 61 & 64-5 © Jeffrey Cody and Mary Day; pp
66 & 71(t) © The Rockwell Group, photos David
Joseph; p 68(t) © The Rockwell Group, photo
Paul Warchol; p 68(b) courtesy MarketPlace
Development; pp 69-70 © Stantec Architecture
in association with ISI-Epstein; p 71(r) © Gail
Satler; pp 72, 74(tl&tr) & 76-7 © Louisa Carter;
p 73 John Oxley Library neg no 60846; p 74(b) ©
Helen Trocholias; pp 78-85 © David Bell; pp
86-95 © Susan Parham.

AD+
pp 98-100 © MoMA, photos Thomas Loof &
Pernille Pederson; pp 101-5 © Alsop Design
Ltd/Roderick Coyne/Alan Lai; pp 108-11 ©
Jonny Muirhead; p 112 © QinetiQ; p 113 © DACS
2005; p 114 © Peter Clarke; p 115 © Tim
Buchman; p 116 © Richard Davies; p 117 ©
Ilana Rabinowitz; pp 118(t), 119(t), 120-22 &
123(tl&b) © Walters and Cohen; pp 118(b) &
119(bl) © Dennis Gilbert; p 119(br) © Dennis
Gilbert/View; p 123(tr) © Walters and Cohen,
photo Daisy Hutchinson; p 124 © Lisa Linder; pp
125-7 Peter A Sellar/KLIK.

Published in Great Britain in 2005 by Wiley-
Academy, a division of John Wiley & Sons Ltd
Copyright © 2005, John Wiley & Sons Ltd, The
Atrium, Southern Gate, Chichester, West Sussex
PO19 8SQ, England, Telephone (+44) 1243 779777
Email (for orders and customer service enquiries):
cs-books@wiley.co.uk Visit our Home Page on
www.wileyeurope.com or www.wiley.com

Subscription Offices UK
John Wiley & Sons Ltd.
Journals Administration Department
1 Oldlands Way, Bognor Regis
West Sussex, PO22 9SA
T: +44 (0)1243 843272
F: +44 (0)1243 843232
E: cs-journals@wiley.co.uk

Printed in Italy by Conti Tipicolor.
All prices are subject to change
without notice.
[ISSN: 0003-8504]

AD is published bimonthly and is available
to purchase on both a subscription basis
and as individual volumes at the following
prices.

Single Issues
Single issues UK: £22.50
Singles issues outside UK: US$45.00
Details of postage and packing charges
available on request.

Annual Subscription Rates 2005
Institutional Rate
Print only or Online only: UK£175/US$290
Combined Print and Online: UK£193/US$320
Personal Rate
Print only: UK£99/US$155
Student Rate
Print only: UK£70/US$110

Prices are for six issues and include
postage and handling charges. Periodicals
postage paid at Jamaica, NY 11431. Air
freight and mailing in the USA by
Publications Expediting Services Inc, 200
Meacham Avenue, Elmont, NY 11003

Individual rate subscriptions must be paid
by personal cheque or credit card.
Individual rate subscriptions may not be
resold or used as library copies.

Postmaster
Send address changes to AD Publications
Expediting Services, 200 Meacham Avenue,
Elmont, NY 11003

Food + the City

Guest-edited by Karen A. Franck

Δ**D**

If clean drinking water and public sanitation were the main obstacles to social progress in the 19th-century city, a healthy diet and access to fresh food for all promises to be one of the hottest issues for the 21st century. The celebrity cook and self-styled social reformer Jamie Oliver has captured the zeitgeist with his Channel 4 programme for British TV 'Jamie's School Dinners'. For over a year, Oliver worked with the dinner ladies of the London borough of Greenwich in a pioneering attempt to bring back freshly cooked meals. Rose Gray, Ruth Rogers' partner in The River Café, is also part of this movement for better school lunches, and has set up a charity to bring trained cooks into schools. Fresh school dinners are being advocated as a means not only of educating children about food, but also of providing inner-city children with vital nutrients that are otherwise missing from their diets, with many of today's most deprived children simultaneously malnourished and obese. This is a haunting spectre of a society in which priorities have somehow been insidiously switched, as a food industry that aggressively markets junk food to children, and the desire to economise on the unit cost of food on the school dinner plate, have somehow gained the upper hand.

On the streets of Western cities, the division between the haves and the have-nots has been made all the more apparent by the gentrification and regeneration of urban areas supported by a burgeoning restaurant and café culture. Just as diverse and fancy food retailers often encourage wealthy neighbourhoods to flourish, lower-income areas can be deprived of the most basic grocery shops and supermarkets selling the full range of fresh foods (see guest-editor Karen Franck's 'Food for the City, Food in the City' on pp 35–42). Such a situation is a complex one where urban fragmentation means that wealthy areas often butt directly onto sink estates, and the type of food available, and thus consumed, by city dwellers can shift from one end of the road to another. So while food has become one of the most potent tools for social progress – with the power to transform city streets as well as the life expectancy of individuals – it can quite conversely become a force for social exclusion: what happens when local shops pitch themselves above the means of the poorer section of the community?

Karen A Franck's issue of *Food + the City* is multifaceted and thoroughly engaging. By drawing on contributors from a wide range of countries and with very different perspectives, she presents no single cultural or social point of view. The positives and negatives of food as a regenerative force in our towns and cities gets in turn talked up and berated. As in her previous issue of Δ (*Food + Architecture*, No 6, Vol 72, 2002), Franck has here displayed a great rigour and stamina in compiling this publication, bringing together contributions that not only excite but also confound our expectations, prompting us to ask – at a telling time – entirely new questions of what exactly the relationship may be between food and the city. Δ

Above
Vegetables by Turnips at
Borough Market, London.

The City as Dining Room, Market and Farm

Above
Grocery store, Hong Kong.
Fresh fruit and produce on
display in outdoor public
spaces enrich sensory
experiences in the city.

Food has been sold on the street ever since people have lived in town settlements. Encouraging social exchange and interaction, the public consumption of food brings vitality and conviviality to urban life. In recent years, the sale of food in upmarket cafés and speciality shops has intensified, becoming a tool of urban regeneration. Here, Karen A Franck, the guest-editor of this issue, introduces the themes behind 'Food + the City' and suggests why architects and planning professionals should pay attention to 'the city's multiple functions as dining room, market and farm'.

On the streets of Istanbul, vendors sell boiled corn, stuffed mussels served with slices of lemon, soft pretzels and even rice pilaf in small plastic glasses; in New York it may be hot dogs, kebabs, egg rolls, roasted chestnuts, and also pretzels – but harder ones. In Seoul, on cool autumn evenings, many vendors appear, all at once, to prepare and cook a wide range of foods right in front of you, often protected from the wind and cold by canvas enclosures. Around the world, for hundreds of years and more, people have purchased (and eaten) food on the street, just as they have purchased meat, fish, cheese, herbs and fresh produce from urban markets, both indoors and out.

Sitting down in a public place to drink or to eat has also existed for centuries from the age-old tradition of informal street-side eateries in China to medival cookshops in inns in the UK to the 16th-century emergence of coffeehouses in the Middle East and then Europe. More elaborate interior design and culinary arrangements emerged with the French invention of the restaurant in the late 18th century. For religious holidays and other special occasions, people have long gathered in public places to eat together. (In medieval times, the cathedral was a site for such events.) In all these ways, food continues to play a highly visible role in public life in cities throughout the world, meeting people's need for sustenance, sociability and entrepreneurship, and generating a sensory-rich feeling of vitality.

While some traditions remain remarkably the same, others change quickly and dramatically. Even though Europe adopted the café, from the Middle East, in the 17th century, the outdoor sidewalk café is a very recent import of the late 20th century, from the Mediterranean to the UK, Scandinavia, the US and Australia.[1] While restaurants have existed for a long time, their number, variety and popularity has increased worldwide since the Second World War due to a number of factors: an increase in the disposable income of many households; the acceptance in many countries of women eating out without the company of men; the fact that people now remain single for longer periods of time; and because more women now go out to work and have less time to prepare family meals at home.

Growing fruit and vegetables within the city limits, or even nearby, disappeared from many Western cities as large-scale agriculture became exclusively a rural activity, with foods being packaged and transported long distances to urban supermarkets. As the many advantages

Top
Street vendor cooking hot dishes, Seoul, South Korea. Many food vendors in Seoul use this kind of collapsible canvas enclosure with plastic windows on the sides.

Right
Vendor's pushcart for boiling and selling ears of fresh corn, Istanbul, Turkey.

of local agriculture are being rediscovered, farmers' markets and the regeneration of public market buildings attract both residents and tourists, helping to regenerate surrounding districts. And urban residents also rediscover the benefits of growing fruits and vegetables themselves in private and community gardens, city farms and allotments.

The public culture of food brings vitality and conviviality to urban life. People come together in public spaces to buy and to eat, and even to grow food, and in these ways, also, to be with others. They may join people whom they already know, finding in restaurants and cafés the space to eat and converse with friends and family that is simply not available in their own small apartments. Or they may simply enjoy the presence of strangers. Eating venues offer what Ray Oldenburg in his *Great Good Place* calls a 'third place' – that is, neither home nor work.[2]

Within the fast pace of life, anonymity and large-scale spaces of the modern city, food

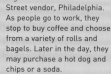

Right
Street vendor, Philadelphia. As people go to work, they stop to buy coffee and choose from a variety of rolls and bagels. Later in the day, they may purchase a hot dog and chips or a soda.

Below
Place Djemaa el Fna, Marrakesh, Morocco. Every evening during the religious month of Ramadan, vendors start preparing food and setting up tables for the meal that breaks the day's fast at sundown.

Top left

Allotment garden, Stockholm, Sweden. Starting in Germany, during industrialisation in the mid-19th century, cities, factories and monasteries provided plots in allotment gardens for poor families to grow food and to keep pigs and chickens. Such gardens became an essential source of food during the world wars. Introduced in Sweden at the beginning of the 20th century, allotment gardens throughout Europe are now more recreational than a matter of food security.

Top right

Spitalfields Market, London. The Horner Market Building (1889), with housing above, once housed a wholesale food and flower market. The interior covered space now houses an arts-and-crafts market, a café, and a food market on Fridays and Sundays. Developers want to build glass blocks inside the market for restaurants, bars and shops, significantly reducing the space available for the present group of small and highly diverse businesses. Despite community opposition, buildings in the western section of the market have been demolished to create space for the construction of office towers.

Bottom left

Stone Street, Lower Manhattan, New York. The departments of city planning and transportation pedestrianised this historic street of 19th-century buildings and restored the street and building facades to their earlier appearance, expecting a range of small businesses to move into the previously vacant and deteriorated shopfronts. To their surprise, the new businesses are all highly successful cafés, bars and restaurants.

Bottom right

Tom's, Prospect Heights, Brooklyn, New York. Owned by a local family since 1939 and a true 'third place', this coffee shop is ever popular with neighbourhood residents and those working nearby, including police officers, and remained open throughout the neighbourhood decline of the 1960s and 1970s.

venues give us a sense of intimacy, a place to pause at an eminently human scale. When the food we eat, grow or buy is local, we also experience a connection to the region, the seasons and the ground we inhabit. Our connection to organic life, within all the abstractions of the modern city, is strengthened. And with the explosion of food products and meals from distant cultures, we find another kind of connection.

Food in the city enriches our everyday sensations of sound, sight and smell through the ways in which it is produced, displayed and consumed. What rich sensory experiences one has walking on the streets of Chinatown in New York or visiting fresh food or fish markets anywhere. What a welcome alternative these are to the many sanitised, sterilised and essentially anaesthetising streets and supermarkets of modern cities. Even just walking by, these sensory experiences are possible and plentiful because the food is not enclosed – neither in tight plastic wrapping nor in shops or restaurants closed and remote from the street. Indeed, a common theme in 'Food + the City' is the blurring of boundaries between inside and out, public and private, eating venue and public circulation that food brings about in street vending, sidewalk cafés, new restaurants in train

stations and airports, and even in public housing estates in Hong Kong.

In many cities, new food-consumption venues are the forerunners of urban regeneration. A lone but quickly popular café or small restaurant, such as Florent in the Meat Packing District in New York, may be followed, quickly or over a period of years, by more restaurants and bars, and also clubs, fashion boutiques, new flats and loft apartments. Elsewhere, the establishment of restaurants, cafés and food markets can be part of a planned redevelopment, as was the incorporation of the largest Whole Foods Market in the US, and some of the most expensive restaurants in New York, into the new Times Warner Center in Manhattan. Either way, by chance or by intention, restaurants and food shops that cater to those with sufficient money to spend on these luxuries are likely to raise rents in the area, forcing out existing businesses and excluding new ones that might serve a different clientele. Municipal governments, keen to encourage consumption by residents and tourists, and to increase the economic wellbeing of the city, often support these trends, perhaps by changing land-use and zoning regulations, as New York and Philadelphia have done, to encourage sidewalk cafés on certain streets.

Nonetheless, the growing gastronomic culture of cities has a range of important economic and health benefits. The great number of restaurants and food outlets provides employment. Opening one's own store or restaurant, although risky, offers opportunities for

Right
Vegetables for sale on the
stairway of the Noryangjin fish
market, Seoul, South Korea.
Selling fresh produce or
prepared foods in public
places is an important source
of income for individuals and
families throughout the world.
Attempts to curtail or forbid
these practices rob people of
their livelihoods and cities
of their liveliness.

Notes
1 For cookshops and early
street-food in the UK, see
Moira Johnston (ed), *London
Eats Out*, Philip Wilson
Publishers (London), 1999. For
histories of the café and
restaurant in Europe, see
Kenneth Kipple and Kriemhild
Conee Ornelas (eds), *The
Cambridge World History of
Food*, Cambridge University
Press, 2000, and Stephen
Mennell, *All Manners of Food*,
University of Illinois Press, 1996.
2 Ray Oldenburg, *Great Good
Place*, Paragon (New York),
1989.
3 For the importance of
vending street food as a
source of household income in
developing countries,
particularly for women, see
Irene Tinker, *Street Foods:
Urban Food and Employment
in Developing Countries*,
Oxford University Press, 1997.

entrepreneurship. Selling cooked food on the
street, as an independent vendor or an employee
of a vending company, turns out to be a very
important source of income worldwide.
Recurring municipal efforts to 'clean up the city'
by curtailing such activity therefore threaten not
only the liveliness of public life, but also the
livelihood of city residents.[3]

The increasing number of farmers' markets in
the poorer neighbourhoods of US cities give
residents access to fresh produce that is simply
not available in neighbourhoods that rely solely
on small cornershops and fast-food chains.
Residents of these neighbourhoods also grow
food which they sell at these markets, and
family-owned farms in the region are able to
stay in business.

Through various programmes, these and
other food enterprises offer training and work
experience for those who are desperately in
need, including immigrants, the formerly
homeless, released convicts and young juveniles.
And growing food and learning to cook and serve
it becomes part of the curriculum in schools
where city children have little if any experience
in these areas. Food is a mechanism of change
in a great variety of ways – for entire
neighbourhoods as well as individuals.

It is time for the architectural and urban design
planning professions to support and enhance the city's
multiple functions as dining room, market and farm.
The Modernist tenets, which too often posited a
segmented and sterile city where dining and shopping
were hidden in interior spaces and where growing
occurred in distant locations, need to be replaced by
the encouragement, through planning and design, of
a true mixing of land uses that incorporates places
(and ways) for growing and selling local produce as
well as for consuming it. Open space need not always
be interpreted as space exclusively for leisure.

It is this kind of design and planning orientation to
the benefits that food can bring to both large-scale and
small-scale urban areas that Brian McGrath, Danai
Thaitakoo, Gil Doron and Susan Parham promote in
this issue. It is the liveliness, conviviality and sensory
experience that open-air markets and informal eating
venues bring to city life that Nisha Fernando, Jeffrey
Cody and Mary Day wish to maintain in the face of the
modernisation projects and city regulations that
threaten them. And all of us join Jane Lawrence,
Rachel Hurst, Gail Satler and Masaaki Takahashi in
discovering the many ways that food in the city is a
boundary-breaker. At the same time, like Louisa
Carter, Jon Binnie and David Bell, we need to notice,
always, who is included and who is excluded, who
benefits and who loses. Δ

Raw, Medium, Well Done: A Typological Reading of Australian Eating Places

Taking their cue from the culinary criteria most often applied to the cooking of a beefsteak, Rachel Hurst and Jane Lawrence develop a taxonomy of design for eating establishments in Australia. They find examples of the 'raw' in Melbourne's buzzing Centre Place, the 'medium' in a chain of Italian restaurants in Adelaide, and the 'well done' at The Restaurant at the Art Gallery of New South Wales in Sydney.

Left
In the close confines of the narrow street and the repetitious trading bays, the dynamic pattern of Centre Place in Melbourne is a familiar one globally. The abundance, diversity and directness of the food on offer add to the sensory stimulation of the place as a whole.

Only 200 years on from its colonisation by Europe, Australia is stereotypically seen as a raw frontier. Yet in terms of digesting the influences of industrialisation, urbanisation and globalisation it is as 'medium' or 'well done' as any other developed country. The architecture, like the cuisine, is a conscious attempt to assimilate both regional specificity and international sophistication. One of the most significant sites illustrating this tension is in the urban realm, where the consumption of architecture and food is played out in the civic places, public spaces and profusion of cafés and restaurants. These places are a physical manifestation of our appetite for urban culture, with their overt appeal to the visual and olfactory senses, and their patent preoccupation with viewing the city as one eats.

The terms 'raw', 'medium' and 'well done' are conventionally used to describe the state of food. The application of these expressions to describe design, while unorthodox, can be useful in a typological analysis of architecture imbuing the reading with a sensory and material focus. Both raw food and raw space carry connotations of simplicity and wholesomeness, yet can concurrently involve a refined composition of elements. Raw foods/spaces embody the most direct and unprocessed state, highly linked to the temporal and regional. Like a well-composed salad, which uses raw and fresh ingredients, the condition suggests immediacy, both of materials and assembly. There are no hidden elements or processes, and the success of the whole relies on its clarity and down-to-earth quality. Similarly, the term 'medium' can be applied to foods and spaces that balance between extremes, while the label 'well done' suggests time-consuming processes that can transform very ordinary ingredients into a refined and concentrated state.

Through the filter of raw, medium and well done, three different groups of urban eating places reveal contemporary attitudes to food, social behaviour and aesthetics in Australia. These examples utilise their relationship to the city for custom and aesthetic. There are, of course, cafés, bistros and restaurants in Australia that are sited to take advantage of nonurban landscapes, such as rural, garden or seaside environments, and there is a strong tradition of eating places that follow the internalised spatial models of pub dining and counter meals. However, the majority of contemporary eating places are distinctly urban creatures, and these specific cases have been selected as clearly indicative of their type, each offering a nuanced interpretation of the sociable and sensual activity of eating in the city.

Raw

The major streets in the heart of Melbourne are connected by an idiosyncratic network of pedestrian lanes and arcades. These lanes, which evolved from

Raw
Above
Skips and crates are casually marshalled off the main thoroughfare of Centre Place, where teenagers loiter below a gritty public art project like players in some hyper-real theatre production.

Right
During its daytime trading hours, Centre Place embodies cosmopolitan richness and density, allowing simultaneous social interaction and engagement in civic life, or alternatively an immersion into anonymity.

mundane service alleys, are now lined with a plethora of small shops and food vendors. The most concentrated collection lines a truncated pedestrian street called Centre Place. While the entrance is heralded by an eccentric wrought-iron arch, the other end is oddly subsumed into the fabric of the city, merging into an unremarkable retail arcade. Compressed between multistorey buildings, the 6-metre-wide street is a dark and unadulterated urban space, wearing the raw scars of graffiti, tagging and disintegrating flyers.

More than 20 small businesses line Centre Place, opening and closing to the street with battered roller shutters. In their unambiguous operation, these steel shutters bring a blunt urbanity to the place – it is exposed, active and convivial during the day, or sealed, impenetrable and inhospitable after hours.

The cafés that dominate this eclectic assortment of shops offer a range of multicultural food choices. Café Aix bases its menu on the classic crêpe, incorporating adventurous crosscultural combinations, from sublime blood plum and burnt sugar, the nursery-food mix of banana and Nutella, to the acquired tastes only Australians might appreciate – Vegemite and Swiss cheese. The shop fit-out makes casual allusion to the simple family bistros of provincial France, with zinc-lined counter top, stacked baguettes and mismatched crockery. Yen Sushi Noodle is an exercise in cultural migration, employing an aesthetic of laced bamboo and the stylised floral arrangements of ikebana as a backdrop for serving folded cartons of stir-fry noodles and disposable plastic *bento* boxes of sashimi and sushi.

These eating places offer a restricted selection of foods; each shop focuses on a particular food type or staple, such as baguettes, noodles or crêpes. Like the limited variety of food they serve, there is a simplicity and repetition to spatial layouts and use. They respond to the proximity of the teeming thoroughfare, by compressing personal space and communality. Roughly 4 metres in width, each hole-in-the-wall crowds kitchen and eating area together in an unruly pattern of cooking and dining. The footpath has been almost entirely appropriated as an eating apron, fringed with rudimentary timber boxes that double as seats, tables and informal bollards so that people are obliged to walk in the street during operating hours. The food from these kitchens is cooked quickly and eaten rapidly.

Raw
Top and right
Footpath and street in Centre Place melt and merge into one another, providing an animated interstitial space for urban consumption.

reflect patterns of daily and seasonal availability. The food available at each shop is never far from its raw state, most ingredients are either whole or discernible as discrete flavours. Similarly, the fit-out of each café projects a raw and elemental quality, through a basic layout of kitchen/counter/dining and a limited palette of robust materials. The recurrent use of stainless steel, tiles, timber and glass, carries connotations of utilitarian function and honesty to materials, though themselves highly processed.

The individual cafés operate like static street vendors, where these chiefly owner-operated and one-off businesses appear to come and go with alacrity in a typologically persistent line-up. Like most raw dishes, which are open to adaptation and assembled at the last minute, the high turnover of youthful enterprises creates an occasional, yet not critical, hiccup in essentially vigorous urban spaces such as this.

Medium

In gastronomy, 'medium' refers to the state between raw and well done, and also to a moderate or average condition; for example, of heat, size or viscosity – a constant and predictable condition with minor variations. In Adelaide, a family of Italian-based cafés illustrates how the concept can be applied to urban eating. Originating as a single Italian restaurant in 1996, Cibô Ristorante Pasticceria established its reputation through premises-baked cakes and *biscotti*, wood-oven cooking, home-made *gelato* and Venetian-temperature espresso. Cibô Espresso is now a modest chain of nine allied businesses dotted strategically around the central business district and liveliest commercial areas of inner and suburban Adelaide. This group has introduced café culture to a city and suburbia previously short-changed for choice in urban eating. Launched by a combination of Italian-born and first-generation Italo-Australians, the concept behind the venture was to provide traditional Italian food using the best local South Australian ingredients in a 'modern yet classical Italian atmosphere that is casual and relaxed' – an effective mediation between two cultures.

All venues have an instantly recognisable urban presence, not because they challenge any architectural norms or built typology, but because of a consistently strong graphic identity projected by signs, umbrellas, street furniture and facade treatments. The bright red-and-white branding of the Cibô image is telling. A balance between arresting graphics and classical clarity, it is designed to appeal broadly to its predominantly middle-class clientele, evoking simultaneously the comfortable exoticism of shiny red sleek Italian icons (think Campari, Ferrari, Olivetti) and the reliable amenity of the modern family restaurant.

A recurring set of spatial and aesthetic precedents, nuanced to respond to specific locations like regional

Diners jostle for space at the counter, share a table or eat on-the-go in the tide of pedestrian traffic. Polite distances between strangers, the usual observances of spatial territory, are dispensed with in the intensity and directness of lunchtime feeding frenzy.

In this highly visible smorgasbord of abundant choice, the patrons are as varied and diverse as the food itself. Strolling in suits, jeans or bohemian chic, consumers peruse the gastronomic offerings without obligation, from the main path. Open to sensory seduction, they are gastronomic *flâneurs*, able to make a considered or capricious choice. Just as big cities allow engagement or anonymity, the intensity of Centre Place operates successfully to support social interaction or pockets of withdrawal.

Associations with the raw can be found in the visibility of the components of the eating experience: kitchens, with all their batterie de cuisine, noise and aromas, are open for scrutiny; food either already prepared, cooked on the spot or assembled in front of customers is displayed without artifice, often at the street face for spontaneous consumption. Simple disposable serving containers are stacked at hand like uncontrived totems. Briskly chalked menu boards, hung or propped to attract attention in the few interstitial spaces between stores,

Raw
Above
Blufish is just one of the multitude of hole-in-the-wall eating places in Centre Place. A lean, cool box lined in stainless steel, it serves fish and chips in crisp white cardboard containers. Its immediate legibility and simple spatial layout are typical of these tiny stores.

variations on a theme, unifies the Cibô group. Using glazed louvred skins and retractable PVC roller shutters they are designed to minimise spatial barriers and maximise visibility. The cafés insinuate themselves into street life, blurring the boundaries between the public space and the interior. In a seamless amalgamation of public and private voyeuristic eating activity, those lingering at outdoor tables, ordering takeaways from the express counter or seated indoors can observe street activity as well as one another.

Internally, most of the cafés replicate the formal quality of the street by using linear arrangements. A generous, glazed display counter runs along one side; an elongated seating banquette and a long communal table face it. The effect of using these uninterrupted joinery elements rather than a predominance of individual chairs and tables is to suppress individual allocation of space in favour of a continuous merging of personal territory, encouraging communality in a subtle replication of the fluid civic quality of the street. As a balance to this overt sociability, a small collection of discrete tables allows for detachment and retreat.

The medium examples balance interior eating spaces and street dining, favouring neither one nor the other and edging, but not invading, the public realm. This is occupational

removed from basic notions of shelter. Another productive reading of the term 'well done' provides an analogy with the meticulous realm of nouvelle cuisine, where each ingredient is painstakingly processed, arranged and composed as part of a carefully considered totality.

The Restaurant, designed by Johnson Pilton Walker in the recent additions to the original neoclassical Art Gallery of New South Wales, epitomises this sophistication of food and design. Encased in a luminous glass box, The Restaurant cantilevers over the public parklands known as the Domain and surrounding city of Sydney like an ethereal acropolis, framing spectacular views of Woolloomooloo Bay and the botanic gardens. One of the few built structures in the green belt, the Art Gallery of New South Wales is a central landmark, yet spatially and ideologically removed from its commercial and secular context.

Unlike Centre Place and Cibô, this eating place is not connected to the street. Entering only during lunchtime, visitors pass along the main promenade of the art museum to reach it. The expansive spaces of The Restaurant reinforce the enfilade planning of the gallery, and the preoccupation with visual clarity and axial sight lines common to conventional gallery design is perpetuated in the lucid quality and layout of the entire area. The terraced floor plane sets up a succession of viewing platforms to other dining areas, the open kitchen and long vistas to the galleries. The glazed skin gives an impressive full-frontal view of the urban environment, where size does matter. The place is an exercise in degrees of transparency on both a micro and macro scale. The attitude to the outside world is idealised and sanitised, possessed through the filter of the invisible casing. This presentation of the city landscape bears similarities with modern commercial food production – the scientifically engineered practices that produce genetically perfect food or, at the macro scale, the cultivated agricultural environments that exist to support urbanity.

Although The Restaurant maintains the museum aesthetic in its use of neutral and natural surfaces, it is devoid of artwork. Canvases are replaced by the subtly shifting panorama of contemporary urbanity, perhaps as an intentional foil to gallery indigestion. Just as the ubiquitous white plate acts as a backdrop for nouvelle cuisine, the container operates as a blank slate for the play of light, space, occupation and culinary interpretation. Similarly, the creative conception and crafting of dishes on the menu is instantly apparent and immediately visual in its appeal.

In the raw and medium examples, food is prepared, advertised visually and selected spontaneously. In the well-done setting the process of ordering is attenuated, informed by mental anticipation and assiduously prepared upon request.

pluralism, supporting both gregarious and private behaviours, in an Antipodean version of the civic and private demarcations of Italian urban life. In design terms, the notion of medium is almost pejorative in a realm where designers seek continually to create the extraordinary. Yet as an evocation of a balance between two extremes, it has currency for designs that are attempting to respond to the typical binaries of inside/outside, private/public, tradition/innovation and simplicity/complexity. With their careful equilibrium of contemporaneity and convention, the Cibô cafés provide both a cultural synthesis and a spatial illustration of the middle ground.

Well Done

In gastronomic terms, 'well done' has a dual connotation. Used most often to describe food that has been thoroughly cooked, it is also used in a more general sense to praise something well conceived and executed. However, it can be ambiguous labelling when applied to the cooking of foods such as meat and vegetables. Consider, for example, the chewy greyness of a piece of steak broiled beyond recognition, or a pile of overcooked carrots, waterlogged and spineless. As an architectural analogy, one might question whether a 'well-done' building can be seen as 'overcooked'. Undeniably, though, there are directions in architecture that rely on highly processed materials and methods to achieve their ends, where the finished work is sophisticated, technologically dependent and far

Medium
Above
Just as the selection of *pasticceria* or antipasto is visible, composed and abundant, the design of the Cibô cafés is legible, precise and generous. All the food is prepared and presented with conscious respect for its local and foreign origins, a visible synthesis of European food traditions and contemporary Australian urbanity.

Like the careful spatial and aesthetic demarcations in the restaurant, the preparation and presentation of food is deliberately metered to heighten the sensory experience. Water, wine, bread and food are each offered as sequential acts of service, orchestrating a hierarchical and articulated approach to the fundamental act of eating.

The maintenance of a clear and ideal state, devoid of clutter, is replicated through the ordered geometry of the restaurant's layout. Linearly segregated by lean benches and stepped tiers, cooking, serving and dining areas are arranged in a gleaming trinity of spaces. Various seating arrangements set up another trilogy, this time for potential social interaction. Patrons can choose discreet tables at the banquette flanking the corridor, the long communal table in full view of entry and kitchen, or a table in the main salon.

The restrained approach in the aesthetic of both food and interior appears economical in means, but not in ends. The apparent simplicity belies the complexity of production, where the austerity is paradoxically achieved through a lavish hand with things unseen – luxurious amounts of space, ample kitchen, the removal of unnecessary accoutrements; and only trimmed, choice cuts of food make it to the table. Reductionist, rarefied and intended for cerebral as well as physical sustenance, this style is the neo-Modernism of haute cuisine.

Reading the Recipe

Associations between food and architecture are increasingly being explored as stimulating metaphors for design and discourse. These alliances are often based on the sensory evocations gastronomy is able to impart to architecture and its connections to place and process.[1] The use of food as a tool for inquiry in architecture foregrounds issues of communality, cultural heritage, ritual and the everyday, commodity and comfort. These associations apply equally if one infuses typological readings with ideas related to food. For example, Cibô's Italian roots become obvious, not through anything immediately discernible as 'Italianate' in the architectural vocabulary, but via the offerings of *pannini*, *chinotto* and *cannoli* on the menu. Prompted by the direct cultural references in the food, one may then recognise the implicit debt to imported modes of spatial and social interaction.

The concepts of raw, medium and well done are terms broad enough to exploit the breadth of

The maintenance of a clear and ideal state, devoid of clutter, is replicated through the ordered geometry of the restaurant's layout. Linearly segregated by lean benches and stepped tiers, cooking, serving and dining areas are arranged in a gleaming trinity of spaces.

Well Done
Top
Aloft in a translucent vantage point, seated on semi-opaque white chairs, diners in The Restaurant at the Art Gallery of New South Wales in Sydney can be spectators to the lunchtime traffic of pedestrians and physical fitness buffs in the public gardens below, or voyeurs of waterfront urban life.

Right
The axial planning, direct sight lines and neutral finishes of The Restaurant seamlessly continue the aesthetic of its host, the Art Gallery of New South Wales. The ordered geometries and minimalist design of fittings and furniture focus attention on the art of the food. A blond veneer box divides the grand table, and provides an elongated screen and regimented array of glossy art books and journals as substitute companions for the lone diner.

Well Done
Above
Colour is pooled in saturated doses at The Restaurant: the Rothko red of the carpet square and the slices of amber Corian act like intense garnishes to a big white dish. An elegant sculptural block hovers above the stairs, doubling as an illuminated divider on one side and an upholstered bench-seat on the other.

gastronomy, yet specific enough to be accessible and evocative. They have obvious perceptual characteristics that are not only tangible, but also able to be interpreted in terms of processes and use, and have a multiplicity of conceptual attachments or meaning. It is the undeniable physical nature of each state that makes them generic enough to have meaning across cultural barriers, where more language-based analogies might fail. Their use as a means of ordering eating places extends the current terms of reference beyond economic-, cultural- and etiquette-based categorisations.

For example, there are humble eating places worldwide, from the Spanish bodegas to the hawkers' stalls of Singapore, which have comparable characteristics of freshly prepared food, limited menus, direct street access and simple floor plans with rudimentary furniture. By defining Centre Place as a raw type, the observed compression of personal space, the

briskness of the trade, the utilitarian finishes and the repetition of basic layout become a manifestation of honest vitality and straightforward sustenance. Subject to changing fashion and food fads, this type can be mercurial in its appearance and disappearance. The medium typing of Cibô, in comparison, reveals a gentler life cycle, the parent restaurant promising to become a modest landmark chronicling, like an inherited recipe, the collective habits and memories of generations of city users.

Despite their different states, all have in common an implicit recognition that an eating place, like a city, is essentially about civitas, about a sense of community through shared activities and behaviour, the urban manners of everyday life in civilised society. Whether it is through an invisible and impermeable skin, a filtered casing of canopies and screens or a complete removal of the boundary between street and interior, these examples temper, but never abandon, the street as a continual source of nourishment. Like Baudelaire's *flâneur*, the definitive gourmand of the metropolis who

Well Done
Above
The Restaurant gives the impression of a truly modern space and cuisine, a-historical, international and highly evolved. The kitchen and cooks are framed as if on a stage for performance art, an active foil to the subdued atmosphere of the dining space.

Notes
1 See, for example, Sarah Wigglesworth, 'Cuisine and architecture: A recipe for a wholesome diet', in Karen Franck (ed), 'Food + Architecture', Ð Vol 72, No 6, Nov/Dec 2002, p 102.
2 Claude Lévi-Strauss, *From Honey to Ashes* (1973) and *The Origin of Table Manners* (1978), trans John and Doreen Weightman, Harper & Row (New York), pp 323 and 495 respectively.

roved the city as a voyeur of urban decorum and richness, the cafés are a contemporary manifestation of our gluttony for urban culture from the raw to the refined.

While a menu can give blatant clues to the typing of an eating place, raw, medium and well-done classifications are not dependent upon the literal presence of food in the architectural brief. Rather than produce a fixed set of rules, the various states are more like general 'performance criteria' that can be applied to the defining typological characteristics of any building type. For example, the observed similarities between the raw places – their immediacy to the street, diminutive size, simplicity of layout and one-off ownership – are not immutable characteristics of all raw places, just as a baguette or picnic can be made many ways, eaten inside or out, with a knife and fork or with the hands. Similarly, well-done places might not be entirely removed from the street,

or employ a minimalist design vocabulary and rely on silver service. They are, however, identifiable by the level of design detail and control of each aspect of the eating experience, in the same way that cordon bleu cooking relies on elevating cooking to a precise art form. Just as cooks interpret recipes according to taste, technique and memory, this system of typing is not rigidly prescriptive. And just as typing is about collections and recollections, food, in whatever state, is part of an immense collection of ingredients, recipes and processes itself, and a catalyst for intensifying memories of common experiences.

Claude Lévi-Strauss, the definitive philosopher on the raw and cooked, hypothesised that cuisine forms a language through which society codes messages and unconsciously reveals its structure.[2] The purpose of using raw, medium and well done is to combine that language with a typological framework to tease out imaginative associations, offsetting otherwise prosaic processes of analysis with an emphasis on the holistic sensory experience of architecture. Ð

TASTE, SMELL AND SOUND

ON THE STREET IN CHINATOWN AND LITTLE ITALY

Like magnets, Chinatown and Little Italy, in Manhattan, attract New Yorkers and tourists alike, who come to eat and browse. The sale of food from street vendors, restaurants, cafés and specialist shops encourages a dynamic street life. Despite the commercial success and headlining in guide books of these districts, city officials the world over regard street vendors as disruptive and unsanitary. Nisha Fernando argues on their behalf, evoking the distinctive sensory experiences they afford.

Stepping out of the subway entrance, I have to adjust my eyes not only to the bright daylight, but also to a very crowded scene. Throngs of people – tourists, street hawkers, customers and traffic police – are all trying to negotiate the sidewalk space, resulting in a rather slow pace. Walking among them, I am stopped short by a deep aroma: the smell of boiling rice. A restaurant on the side has its door open. A few steps further on, another strong smell is in the air: egg rolls, fried chicken and *lo mein*. A vendor stands behind a small pushcart at the edge of the sidewalk, efficiently preparing food while calling out 'one dollar, one dollar'. On sniffing the air, people line up to buy the freshly prepared, delectable 'fast food'. Next, my eyes catch sight of the bright colours of a fruit-and-veg stall – yellow mangoes and finger bananas, red lychees, brown spiky durians, young white coconuts, purple aubergines and dark-green vegetables, all arranged neatly under a large multicoloured umbrella. My senses keep being filled with more information on food, telling me the unmistakable: I am in Chinatown, New York City.

Food and the Street

A major magnet that draws people to urban open public space is the opportunity to enjoy food. In addition to satisfying hunger and thirst, food plays an important role in urban life, as an attractive way to relax, read, socialise and people-watch. It has also become a distinctive part of the urban lifestyle, and outdoor restaurants and cafés mushroom in cities for this very reason. A recent proposal of the New York Department of City Planning recommends earmarking particular streets for outdoor-café activities as a way to encourage people to enjoy the public life of the city.[1] The proponents of the project expect that while sitting in outdoor cafés, people will also be able to enjoy the many sights and sounds of the surrounding city simultaneously with goings-on within the café. Enclosed restaurants, physically separated from the street, are unable to offer the same, sensory-rich experience.

But it is not only outdoor restaurants and cafés that provide public spaces via food. In cities where pedestrian activities are a way of life, streets are filled with vendors selling a plethora of foods from mobile carts and smaller pushcarts. Movable carts allow vendors to station themselves easily in strategic public places popular with pedestrians; for example, hot-dog vendors in front of museums and by Central Park in New York City, kebab vendors, roast-nut vendors and soda sellers. Sometimes these vendors also move along the streets from one place to another. Whilst street food-vending contributes to the small-scale retail economy and employment rate of a city, it also generates an interesting experience for urban pedestrians and creates a distinctive ambience for the urban landscape.

Streets in Chinatown display a dynamic urban character through a variety of open shops, restaurants,

temples, street vendors, street artists and people distributing flyers. Pedestrians experience urban life on the street more than they are able to in indoor shops. A striking feature of this street life is the opportunity to view, purchase and consume a wide variety of food. Restaurants offer a huge range of region-based Chinese food. Though enclosed, they often entice the passer-by with prominent displays of food, from roast duck to bakery products, behind large glass windows. In addition, part of the kitchen is placed at the front of the restaurant, next to the window, so that pedestrians can see the cooking in progress. Bakery shops also visually link the sidewalk to the interior: large transparent glass windows display an array of baked goods as well as different types of tea and

fruit drinks, and colourful, enticing posters on the entrances inform passers-by of what is available inside.

A more informal setting for the consumption of food is the sidewalk itself. Vendors on Canal Street fry egg rolls and chicken wings, and prepare vegetable fried rice, which are then placed in small polystyrene boxes for the consumers eagerly waiting in line. Some sell exotic and colourful fresh fruits such as lychees, guavas, papayas, Asian mangoes and finger bananas. People buy young coconuts and sip their water under the shade of the vendor's large umbrella. Another sells vegetables regional to Asia – Chinese aubergine, bok choi, Asian spinach, squash, sour gourds – and Chinese customers gather round and barter noisily with the vendor.

Another vendor stands behind a very small pushcart and bakes small Chinese cakes while curious pedestrians look on. Yet another sits behind his merchandise and eats lunch from a small polystyrene box just purchased from a neighbouring vendor. Food is sold buildingside as well as kerbside, creating an interesting maze of gastronomic activity. There are also numerous tourists tasting fruits, drinking exotic tea with tapioca, and munching on roast nuts whilst walking from one gift shop to another. Foods in Chinatown are abundant, and a big part of the overall experience of the place.

Crossing Canal Street to Mulberry Street, the ambience changes dramatically. A colourful woven garland made of shiny material hanging above the street pronounces: 'Welcome to Little Italy.' There are

Open shops selling Chinese herbs, dried fish and dried food display their goods in boxes on the sidewalk. These open displays entice people to touch, smell and even sample. Those simply passing by without actually buying any food are also connected to the merchandise through their visual, olfactory and gustatory senses.

no street vendors selling hot food or exotic fruits. Here, the sidewalks are neatly lined with large, colourful umbrellas, under which rows of café tables and chairs are set up adjacent to the restaurants. Visitors can enjoy a wide variety of Italian foods, chosen from menu stands displayed along the sidewalk, and sit down at the café tables to do so at their leisure. Waiters stand on the sidewalk, greeting pedestrians and welcoming customers. On an ordinary day, the ambience here is more orderly, in sharp contrast to the street life just a block away in Chinatown. However, during summer festivals the area is closed to traffic, becoming a place of vigorous pedestrian food activities, including *gelato* stalls and more outdoor cafés. In both contexts, food and the street are strongly linked, forming lively social settings.

Smell, Taste and Sound
In addition to the visual character it creates, the food on the streets of both Chinatown and Little Italy generates other sensory experiences.

In Chinatown, along Mott Street, a restaurant door opens and pedestrians are immediately surrounded by smells of roast meat and fried rice. Overripe and strong-smelling fruits such as durian emit an interesting odour. And outside a fishmonger, with its shopfront wide open, the sidewalk is lined with wooden crates of live crabs and lobsters, as well as tanks full of live fish. Next door, passers-by experience the

aroma of freshly baked cakes. And on Grand Street, open shops selling Chinese herbs, dried fish and dried food display their goods in boxes on the sidewalk. These open displays entice people to touch, smell and even sample. Those simply passing by without actually buying any food are also connected to the merchandise through their visual, olfactory and gustatory senses.

Sounds particular to the Chinatown district accompany the array of different food smells here – metal spoons and pans banging together, the hissing sounds of deep-frying, street vendors calling out prices in English, Chinese customers bargaining feverishly in Cantonese, and the general chatting on the street.

In Little Italy, restaurants and cafés line up along the street, producing continuous yet subtly changing food smells that fill the nostrils of passers-by. Doors are wide open to the street and, in good weather, patrons sit at tables on the sidewalk, immediately in front of restaurants, under large umbrellas or wide entrance awnings. Cafés are separated from pedestrians and the rest of the sidewalk only by a step, iron railing, hanging plants, planters with Italian cypress, or a carpet demarcating the café area. Patrons enjoy savoury Italian foods – spaghetti, garlic bread, pizza and seafood. There is also the smell of coffee emanating from smaller cafés, and of cigars lingering around on the sidewalk. Italian music, the clatter of wine glasses and the lively chatter of diners together present an interesting cacophony of sounds.

All this is in striking contrast to the supermarket shopping experience, where foods are often contained in plastic, glass or paper, and prices are fixed, and where the interior space is usually smell-free with minimal noise.

Culture and Sensory Experience
Specific foods and food-consumption practices at street level generate sensory qualities particular to certain cultures. The smell of egg rolls identifies Chinatown as much as the Italian music in Little Italy's cafés identifies that district. Similarly, city streets in Colombo, Sri Lanka, portray an urban character shaped by culture-specific food-related activities. In general, Sri Lankan people prefer to eat indoors, away from public view. Thus, despite the year-round warm climate, there are few sidewalk cafés or outdoor restaurants at street level. Nevertheless, the streets are filled with people buying takeaway fast food (especially at lunch- and dinner times), region-specific fruits, vegetables, fresh fish, herbs and spices, nuts, candy, ice cream and soft drinks, to the accompaniment of the loud cries of their vendors. Shops, similar to those in Chinatown, are wide open to the sidewalk, occupying parts of it, and display a wide range of foods. Pedestrians can readily touch, smell and taste before deciding to purchase. They bargain with shopowners in

Top
Mulberry Street, Little Italy, New York. Some of the seating of this outdoor café is located directly on the sidewalk, with the remainder partially separated physically, yet visually connected to the sidewalk.

Right
Mulberry Street's sidewalk cafés are separated from pedestrian paths only by a short railing or a step. The cafés use space in a flexible manner; some adapt to the narrow space under awnings, while others extend their space all the way to the street.

Bottom left
Mulberry Street, Little Italy. Pedestrianised street during a summer festival. The many food vendors add to the vibrant quality of festival activities.

Bottom right
Galle Road, Colombo, Sri Lanka. Shop with a wide variety of dry and fresh foods, open to the street. An informal sociable mood is created as passers-by are able to touch, feel and sometimes taste the foods on offer.

a friendly manner and chat with fellow consumers, creating a convivial atmosphere.

Colombo's street markets fill the sidewalks with fresh farm produce, meat and seafood, and traditional sweetmeats. The freshness of the food and cheaper prices attract crowds of people to these pedestrianised areas, which also become social spaces where neighbours and friends meet and gossip. Small restaurants (*hoatal* or *bath/thosai kadey* in Sinhala), with their wide doors open to the sidewalk, display a variety of baked candy, breakfast dishes, and curries of the day in enclosed glass cases, with hanging bunches of bananas under the awnings. Typical of these restaurants are the sounds of loud ethnic music, the clatter of china and chatter of patrons, and the smells of food and incense, which can be experienced all at once.

The cultural specificity of food activities produces very different olfactory aspects and contributes significantly to the culture-specific character of urban streets. At the same time, in all three cultural contexts listed above – Chinatown, Little Italy and Colombo – food acts as a medium that connects the pedestrian with the indoors, and attracts more pedestrians to the activities on the street. Interestingly, eating on the street is an activity somewhat frowned upon in Sri Lanka, while the very same activity is common in New York City, even defining its urban character.

Towards Enriching Cities

In many cities around the world, the culture of food activities and crowds of consumers on the sidewalk – often blocking the easy passage of others – is the subject of some controversy. Some believe that sidewalks should be kept orderly, clean and free of crowded gatherings. They also suggest that sidewalks must be devoid of chaotic and cluttered sights, confounding sounds and strong odours. However, although the intention here is to create convenient, safe and unobstructed thoroughfares, such streets are often empty of pedestrians since people have no reason or opportunity to stop, linger, touch, smell or chat. Ironically, people pass by in a hurry, or never even use the very streets that are expected to be orderly, 'aesthetically pleasing', more 'sanitary' and 'cleaner'.

It can certainly be argued that 'chaotic' streets smelling of food are not attractive to everyone; for example, some people are offended by the smell of raw fish and bothered by the constant calls of vendors. Yet the examples of Chinatown, Little Italy and Colombo

Notes
1 *Small Sidewalk Cafés Project*, Department of City Planning, New York City, 2004.
2 S Mazumdar, 'Sense of place considerations for quality of urban life', in NZ Gulersoy and A Ozsoy (eds), *Quality of Urban Life: Policy vs Practice*, Istanbul Technical University, 2003.

At a time when Western cities are becoming increasingly multicultural, understanding the role and relevance of food activities in different cultural enclaves is a crucial contribution towards a more inclusive decision-making process in urban planning. Rather than stereotyping cultures, this approach may generate more appreciative perceptions among urban consumers.

demonstrate that streets that are 'chaotic' are widely patronised by pedestrians – an indication that food activities do in fact attract a diverse range of people. On the other hand, streets that lack much activity – food experiences included – become sterile and devoid of life.

The question, then, is to identify whom city streets cater for and what public activities should or should not take place on them. At this point, the role of food should be considered with the public in mind, as well as its role in enhancing the identity and temperament of a city.

Food experiences enrich our perceptions, understanding and appreciation of city streets. 'Sensoryscapes' that create rich urban experiences through 'visualscapes', 'olfactoryscapes' and 'soundscapes'[2] sharpen our senses. In addition, they signify specific cultures. At a time when Western cities are becoming increasingly multicultural, understanding the role and relevance of food activities in different cultural enclaves is a crucial contribution towards a more inclusive decision-making process in urban planning. Rather than stereotyping cultures, this approach may generate more appreciative perceptions among urban consumers. And, rather than repeating the same design of sterile unused streets, leaving space for spontaneous and culture-laden street life has the potential to generate an exciting public social life in our cities. The focus must be on making urban streets flexible to their users under regulations other than those that overspecify land uses and apply strict zoning codes, so that users of different cultures can then modify, add to or change the streets in ways appropriate to their society and culture. ᴆ

The New and the Rare:

Luxury and Convenience in Japanese Depa-chika

Above

Maison Mikuni, Tobu department store, Ikebukuro 1-11-1, Toshima-ku, Tokyo, Koichi Shimizu, 2002
Maison Mikuni is located in the basement of the Tobu department store. There are some 240 shops on this floor. Showcases in *depa-chika* are usually rectangular, so this one, with its exceptional shape and French atmosphere, is especially appealing to customers.

In the face of economic adversity, the food sections of Japan's department stores have prospered, attracting large numbers of customers with their fresh produce, luxurious dishes and buzzing market-like atmospheres. Masaaki Takahashi describes how these *depa-chika* have not only met the demand for prepared foods among busy working people, but have also stimulated it. Selling the finest delicacies, they tempt their customers with rare items that are often bought for their novelty value alone.

Amid the bright lights and lavish food displays, middle-aged women converge upon a small shop, the Troisgros bakery and delicatessen, in the basement of the Odakyu department store in Shinjuku, one of the busiest shopping areas in Tokyo. 'The pastries have finished cooking,' announces a saleswoman. In the blink of an eye, a line forms and a pastry-purchasing frenzy ensues. The cashier madly hits the bleeping register keys while pastries fly out of the store. When they sell out, the shoppers vanish and the store returns to its former tranquillity. This French bakery, well known among gourmets, sells freshly made pastries a set number of times throughout the day. People come from afar, by train, to buy popular products limited by region or time of sale, creating a common phenomenon in *depa-chika* – the basement food markets of Japanese department stores.

Consisting of various shops of different sizes and displaying different designs, all leased by the department store to individual tenants, *depa-chika* bring together a vast array of foods from fresh vegetables, fish and meat, liquors, teas and desserts to cooked items for lunch and dinner. Their activity peaks at rush hour when people pack the subways. A broad range of tastes and prices is apparent. Some *depa-chika* sell high-end cooked foods for New Year (known as *osechi ryori*), prepared at venerable Kyoto gourmet restaurants. One container, the size of a hatbox, may cost $10,000. At the same store, small booths may offer light, quickly cooked foods, such as *tako-yaki* (small grilled flour balls, filled with bits of octopus and vegetables) sold at night. Recently, eat-in spaces and cooking demonstrations have been coupled with the food for sale.

Recent History

After Mistukoshi, a kimono shop in existence since 1673, opened the first Western-style department store in 1904, department stores led Japanese urban culture in adopting Western architecture and products. When Western food was still a rarity, they built high-class Western restaurants and even sported small amusement parks on their roofs. They housed special bands, theatre troupes, theatres, passenger boats and museums, some of which are still in existence today.

It was during the Taiso era (1912–26) that department stores started selling food, but the collecting of foodstuffs on the basement level did not begin until the 1970s. Then, in 1982, the Ikebukuro branches of the Seibu department store christened *shokuhinkans* (meaning buildings for 'foodstuffs', or *shokuhin*), on their basement floors. These stores proved that customers would flock to the renovated, high-end spaces with a full stock of food, and many department stores refurbished their own grocery floors, laying the foundations for today's *depa-chika*. Though the market for foodstuffs was badly hit by the collapse of the economic bubble in the 1990s, the gourmet boom several years later once again increased people's interest in prepared dishes (including ones from luxury delicatessens). And it is this renewed popularity of the ready-prepared dish that helped stimulate the present boom.

In the 1980s, supermarkets and shopping malls threatened the position of the department stores, and the long recession of the 1990s rubbed salt into their wounds. The profits of the department-store business plummeted, and the number of provincial department stores near to bankruptcy is still increasing. Department stores still hold onto their brand-name power in seeking out new areas of business, but even so the brisk business at basement level far surpasses that on the other floors. According to statistics from the Japanese Ministry of Economy, Trade and Industry, in 1994 the total sales of all products in Japanese domestic department stores stood at 11 billion yen, gradually dropping to 9.5 billion yen by 2001. However, sales of foodstuffs and restaurant meals have held steady since their 1994 level of around 2.5 billion yen. *Depa-chika* sales total roughly 20 per cent of overall department-store sales.

According to Kenji Ibuki, chief of the development marketing group for Takashimaya's subsidiary Toushin Kaihatsu, which handles product development on behalf of the Tamagawa Takashimaya Shopping Centre in Tokyo: 'The phenomenon of department stores emphasising the importance of food seems to be expanding worldwide. The *depa-chika* will cease to be a phenomenon peculiar to Japan, but will spread throughout the world's department stores in much the same way that the animation characters of Japan became disassociated with nationality and spread to become accepted in the West.'

Traditional and Contemporary Customs

Grocery areas of department stores originally targeted customers buying food as gifts. The Japanese have a custom of buying and sending gifts in accordance with the seasons, and this became a major source of income for the department stores, with foodstuffs making up a large percentage of such gifts. Summer gifts, called *ochugen*, and winter gifts, known as *oseibo*, have particular importance. Japanese do not only exchange these gifts between one another; the gifts also carry a significant social function when exchanged between companies. And when visiting someone's house, Japanese often bring treats, referred to as *omiyage* and often bought from department stores. Purchases of these presents also rode the wave of the 'gourmet boom', with ingredients also starting to become popular gifts.

In recent years, Japanese women have taken a more active role in society outside the home and now depend on the purchase of prepared foods. The majority of Japanese men tend to avoid not only cooking, but also housework in general, a tendency more prominent among older generations. Whether single or married, women have started buying ready-prepared dishes (*sozai*) at *depa-chika* in order to save time. In addition, the tradition of families dining together as a group has diminished and, as family members now tend to eat separately, storable premade dishes are now more convenient. Further, the gourmet boom has meant that the number of single people (especially women) who enjoy spending lavish sums on delicious food has also increased. The Japanese use the buzzword *puchi-zeitaku*, or 'petite luxury', to refer to living frugally most of the time but with the occasional splurge on something special – a popular way to fulfil the desire for a little of the good life.

Unlike the uniform and predictable displays at supermarkets, *depa-chika* products are vividly displayed; there is a feeling of vitality and a greater number of staff. And, also in contrast to self-service supermarkets, *depa-chika* staff actively communicate with customers. Many people, especially the elderly, want a break from reality, to go to a bustling place where they can experience human contact. At the perimeter of Japan's cities, local shopping streets, called *shotengai* – near stations, temples and shrines – once functioned as such places of communication for residents, but with the widespread development of supermarkets, convenience stores, discount stores and housing complexes, many *shotengai* have deteriorated. However, whilst shopping centres and supermarkets have mainly driven out the *shotengai*, in using *depa-chikas* people are still – albeit subconsciously – seeking out these 'good old' shopping areas, the cheerful shouting of the *depa-chika* salespeople evoking the feeling of the *shotengai*.

The Search for the New and the Rare

In gathering many tasty titbits from around the world, *depa-chika* skilfully latch onto the psyche of the Japanese consumer's fervour for new products and interesting new stores. For example, they sell foods unknown to the Japanese and hybrid desserts made from a peculiar combination of Western and Eastern

'Limited availability' sums up the roots of the popularity of the *depa-chika*. Products are limited to a certain season, to a certain number produced, to the select stores where they are sold, and to select times when they can be bought.

ingredients. They rotate these items with the seasons, such changes preventing customers from tiring of the foods. Tokyo's Printemps Ginza department store, as the name indicates, previously specialised in French-style atmosphere and merchandising. Now one could almost call it 'Pri-Chika' (Printemps Basement), since the basement food section famously sells rare desserts and new products one after another.

The *depa-chika* stores carry world-renowned products (managers often find ones by iconic chefs and pastry cooks to attract customers who wish to buy and eat food from famous shops), as well as lesser-known products. In the Tokyo area, some department stores create partnerships with famous European restaurants and grocers and establish local branches. *Depa-chika* managers search frantically for delicious products, and on hearing of a trendy or reputable establishment inevitably check it out. If products are appropriate for their department store, they passionately entice owners to become tenants and dispose of stores no longer in vogue. In addition, Japanese department stores renovate their grocery sections once every few years, fervently altering the layout and switching tenants around in short cycles.

'Limited availability' sums up the roots of the popularity of the *depa-chika*. Products are limited to a certain season, to a certain number produced, to the select stores where they are sold, and to select times when they can be bought. Examples of this are freshly made pastries or dumplings, which often sell out in a very short period of time. The Japanese are willing to go to great lengths to purchase whatever is desirable, and willingly wait in line. Often, this lining up at the point of sale attracts the attention of other customers – out of curiosity or simply because they are unable to ignore the queue. This is not dissimilar to the reactions of people who, when they spot a line of young people snaking out of a ramen shop or revolving sushi bar with a good reputation, show off their perseverance by waiting outside for up to an hour or more.

Uoriki Fish Market, Tamagawa Takashimaya Shopping Centre, Tamagawa City, Tokyo
Designer: Luckland, 2003

In 1969, the Tamagawa Takashimaya Shopping Centre opened as the first suburban-style shopping centre in Tamagawa City, in the west of Tokyo. It is not a department store, but under the umbrella of Takashimaya, the mall holds the halo of the department-store brand. The floor space exceeds 5,000 square metres, making it one of the largest shopping spaces in the capital. From the outset, it was modelled as a mid-size, upmarket American-style shopping mall.

In 1977, the south annex was erected and, in 2003, renovated and expanded with further emphasis on architectural design. Takashimaya chose Tadasu Ohe, a famous architect, as project designer – an unusual move since Japanese department stores usually use in-house architects. Ohe designed the main building with many glass and white planes to express transparency.

Externally, it resembles a high-end department store, and the management uses *depa-chika* business tactics. During the renovation, the grocery section was enlarged by 50 per cent with the addition of 30 shops.

Established in 1930, Uoriki sells fresh fish and sushi, and has many branches in commercial buildings. The design company Luckland originally designed refrigerated showcases, and designed the store to look like a small fish market. Japanese people love to shop in such a small area, as it reminds them of a small market or traditional *shotengai*. They also like to buy things at shops where they can communicate with sales staff and vendors in a bustling and colourful atmosphere. This project is quite large in floor area compared with other shops, and the 'shop in shop' atmosphere is very effective. Clear showcases impress customers, and the designers paid particular attention to displaying fish attractively, controlling the smell of fish with a spray of ozone water to express cleanliness and a sanitary environment. In this sense, it differs from the *shotengai* environment.

Above
Uoriki Fish Market, Tamagawa Takashimaya Shopping Centre, Tamagawa City, Tokyo, Luckland, 2003
Based in Hachioji City in Tokyo, Uoriki has 41 shops. Here, steel plates and tiles were used to express cleanliness, a design closer to that of a Western fish shop than a traditional Japanese one.

Right
The sushi-bar area of the Uoriki Fish Market.

Above
Kakiyasu Dining at Tsuruya-hyakkaten, Kumamoto, Kyushu Island, Hisanobu Tsujimura and Shuri Takeuchi, 2001
Light wall panels and the colourful floor pattern create a 'salad of colours' in the eat-in corner.

Kakiyasu Dining, Tsuruya department store, Kumamoto, Kyushu Island
Designers: Hisanobu Tsujimura and Shuri Takeuchi, 2001
Established in 1871, Kakiyasu, based in Mie Prefecture, has expanded into three types of chains: Western-style prepared dishes (Kakiyasu Dining), Japanese-style prepared dishes (Gochisoya Kakiyasu) and Chinese-style prepared dishes (Shanghai Deli). It made its name with its 'Shigureni Beef', called so after a process of raising cows that has been handed down in Mie Prefecture for 250 years. The chains stand alongside the salad store RF1 as nationally popular *depa-chika* shops.

In Kumamoto, the store in the basement of the Tsuruya department store features an eat-in space coupled with an open kitchen. Designer Hisanobu Tsujimura comments: 'Since you have only a moment to communicate the store's message to the many people that come to *depa-chikas* every day, we made a space that has an instant impact even from afar.' He adds that he aimed to incorporate features to make an interior where customers felt they could be buying shoes or clothing, but were actually buying premade dishes. He especially focused on colour, temperature and lighting to bring out a feeling of cleanliness and warmth. 'When the job request came, I went to research some *depa-chikas*, and many of them just display their goods. I was surprised to see that many did not pay particular attention to style. I wanted to express, through the *depa-chika* interior, that you can enjoy food culture. I hope this gives more people a hint as to how to make their lifestyles feel richer.'

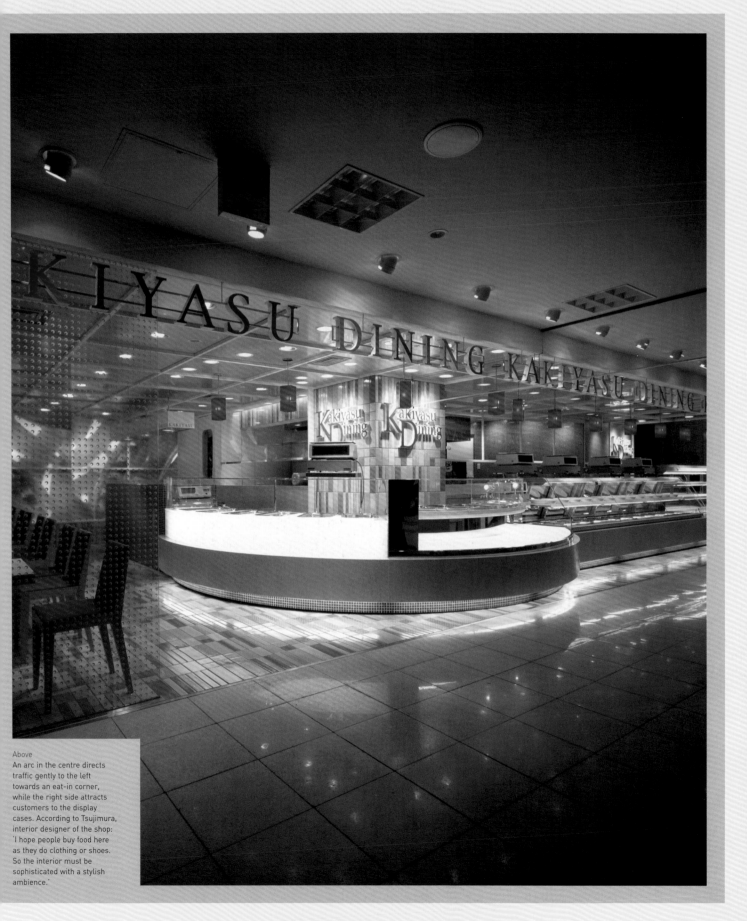

Above
An arc in the centre directs traffic gently to the left towards an eat-in corner, while the right side attracts customers to the display cases. According to Tsujimura, interior designer of the shop: 'I hope people buy food here as they do clothing or shoes. So the interior must be sophisticated with a stylish ambience.'

Boulangerie & Patisserie Maison Mikuni , Tokyo
Designer: Koichi Shimizu, 2002
Maison Mikuni sells eat-in prepared dishes
(*sozai*) at a chain of stores, with spaces in
Shinjuku's Odakyu and Ginza's Matsuya
department stores and a substantially larger
space in Ikebukuro's Tobu department store.
Tobu targets the type of clientele that Mikuni
appeals to. The Mikuni space, in the back of the
store, is conveniently next to a wine shop where
customers can buy wine to drink while eating-in
at Mikuni. Shimizu, the project's interior
designer, used an authentic French style to
represent European style. He combined a French
café with a delicatessen, which makes the most of
the advantageous location at the back of the food
floor. A Tiffany store operates out of an upper floor,
and this is kept in mind in the refined store-design
of the *depa-chika*.

The chef, Seizo Mikuni, created the Mikuni brand.
Deciding to becoming a chef at the age 15, by the
age of 20 he was head chef at the Swiss Embassy
in Japan. As the first Japanese chef to enter the
Chambre Syndicate de la Haute Cuisine Française,
he is widely recognised, and *depa-chika* managers
are always on the lookout for such figures. ◬

Food for the City, Food in the City

Karen A Franck notes that the luxury of eating and food shopping in slick new spaces often comes at the cost of losing more ethnically diverse small businesses. When we focus on this aspect of food and the city, though, we may lose sight of food in all its diversity – as grown as well as consumed, as available or not available to those in poorer neighbourhoods. Viewing food as a system, even an urban system, brings many needs and opportunities to the fore.

Above
At the Union Square Greenmarket in New York, open year-round, four days a week, regional farmers sell fresh produce, food products, meat and fish, plants and flowers. The market's success has stimulated renovation of the square, and revitalisation of the surrounding neighbourhood, including the establishment of many high-end restaurants. A new Whole Foods Market opened in an adjacent former department store in spring 2005.

Well-heeled urbanites flock to the newest restaurant designed by a hip architect and widely reviewed for its food and its interior design. Residents wait eagerly for the relocation of a well-known speciality food store in Greenwich Village or the opening of a new Whole Foods store at Union Square. In my own Brooklyn neighbourhood, within just a few years, three new restaurants, a café and a café/bar opened on a single block, while one local supermarket, once a bit dreary and worn, rebuilt its shelves at an elegant diagonal angle to the street, giving front-row display to imported beers.

Every day I witness this culinary evidence of urban regeneration and gentrification with contradictory feelings of pleasure and dismay. I enjoy the more luxurious venues, even just walking by, but I fear the loss of economic and ethnic diversity of both residents and eateries that is the hallmark of urban neighbourhoods. How relieved I am that the well-loved take-out store selling Jamaican beef patties and coconut bread is still there, as is the low-cost Spanish restaurant specialising in chicken, rice, beans and plantains. Although I eat in them as

infrequently as in the new venues, they remain precious symbols of what the neighbourhood still is.

Here But Not Here, Here But Not There
The exploding gastroculture of restaurants and food stores, apparent in so many neighbourhoods throughout New York City, is well chronicled in the popular press. All the attention to the consumption of food (and its studied preparation at home) has put some aspects of food 'on the table' – aspects that make food in the city appear primarily, if not exclusively, a matter of luxury, specialised tastes and urban gentrification through food stores and eateries. Other life-sustaining aspects of food remain nearly invisible – in education, urban design, planning and architecture.

The near invisibility in US cities of food as grown is not surprising given the strict segmentation and sanitisation of land uses that Modernist zoning has adopted and enforced. We desire and create urban 'open space' and encourage a range of activities in it, but, in official plans, such activities do not include farming or raising animals, or even selling fresh produce. (In fact, agricultural uses may be forbidden by law in some residential areas, particularly in suburban locations.) We may view the urban agriculture that is now taking place over large tracts of vacant land in Detroit with alarm, as further evidence of the city's serious decline.

These efforts are examples of grass-roots initiatives to establish community gardens in space that is left over or derelict, and that may later be threatened by redevelopment. And, until recently, 'redevelopment' meant the destruction or conversion of produce markets with little thought given to temporary arrangements for farmers' markets. A powerful vision of the modern city once emphasised cleanliness to the point of sanitisation, abstraction to the point of the removal of all signs of the messiness of everyday life. In the 1980s, in the redevelopment of downtown Newark into office towers connected by skywalks, a long-standing and thriving outdoor fish and produce market was replaced by a parking lot: this in a city devastated by the ongoing loss of local businesses, a city that lacked supermarkets or other venues where residents could purchase fresh food.

A sharp and powerful dichotomy between what is considered urban and what is rural has also served to hide, from urban residents and professionals, the many interconnected activities that make up a 'food system'. The production of food is deemed 'agricultural'; agriculture is assumed to happen in rural areas and hence becomes a matter of rural policy, distinct and treated independently from urban policy and from urban problems (such as housing, transportation, crime and so on). Because of this division in thinking, planners literally do not see the 'chain of activities connecting food production, processing, distribution, consumption as waste management'.[1] In addition, because for many urban residents food is always available in stores and restaurants, they have little reason to be concerned about its accessibility or affordability. Further, the ease with which food is produced, preserved, delivered and made continuously available makes the great distance it travels, and the loss of local farmland, equally invisible. In these two senses, food is just 'there'.

Food is invisible in cities in a third and more literal manner: full-scale grocery stores and supermarkets are simply absent from many low-income neighbourhoods. Small corner stores offer packaged foods, possibly onions and apples and a meagre handful of other, often old fruits and vegetables, but a full range of sodas, candy and chips. These items come at a higher price and are less nutritious than supermarket foods. Such poorer neighbourhoods also sport Chinese takeout and fast-food restaurants that are similarly costly without being nutritious. Not only do residents spend an exceedingly high proportion of their income on housing, the money they do (and often do not) have left does not give them access to affordable, healthy food. Without cars, they cannot easily reach locations where such food is for sale.

Putting Food on the Table

Some of the connections that comprise the dense network of food systems have been recognised. For instance, in the US the food connection between the city and the surrounding region has been acknowledged and supported (if not saved) through the establishment of farmers' markets in urban locations, beginning in the 1970s. An example of this is the very successful Greenmarket in New York. Started in 1976, the programme now operates and manages 47 open-air farmers' markets in all five boroughs, giving small family farmers opportunities to sell their produce and products to New Yorkers, and thereby helping to preserve farmland in the region and improve urbanites' access to fresh food.

Urban residents across the US are also forming food-buying clubs to purchase vegetables from regional farms during the harvest season, receiving whatever the farmers produce that week. The community-supported agriculture (CSA) is basically a subscription to weekly produce. Currently there are about a thousand CSA groups in the US, 28 of which are in New York.

Interest among middle-class urbanites in food grown locally and organically has contributed to the success of

Top
Customer Maxine Daniel with her granddaughter and former mobile market coordinator Anushka Baltes. Two days a week, the mobile market, sponsored by People's Grocery, makes scheduled stops at between four and six locations in West Oakland, California. From the truck, residents can purchase produce grown by local farmers and healthy packaged goods, all at affordable prices.

Bottom
Farmers' markets are also popular in upmarket suburban areas, as in this parking lot next to the train station in Bernardsville, New Jersey, which hosts a market every Saturday morning from May to November. It is now common practice for urban designers to include this kind of market in proposals for transit-oriented development in communities throughout the state.

Top
Edible School Yard, Berkeley,
California. This single-acre
asphalt site next to Martin
Luther King Jr Middle School
has been transformed into a
lush and highly productive
fruit-and-vegetable garden.
Two to three class sessions, of
30 students each, are held in
the garden each school day.
Meeting in a circle, students
choose which jobs they wish
to do. Groups of students also
cook meals which they eat
together.

Above
Rolling carts and panels with
hooks in the tool shed give
easy, organised access to
boots, shovels and gardening
gloves for 30 children. Another
circle of hay bales gives a
shaded spot for classes to
meet under the oak tree. A new
project is the construction of a
dining commons where fresh
organic school lunches that
students and teachers can eat
together will be served.

farmers' markets and increased purchasing
of local produce by restaurants. The question
remains how this link, between fresh food and
the middle-classes, affects those who have
much less income and live in neighbourhoods
that may not have even a single supermarket,
where children are growing up with little
experience of home-cooked meals or sitting
down at a family meal together.

The challenge for those working to increase
'food security' is how to bring local fresh
produce to the tables of these families. One
answer is to establish farmers' markets in low-
income neighbourhoods and, at the market, to
hold cooking demonstrations and workshops
on meal preparation and nutrition. (Being able
to buy the produce is only the first step in getting
food to the table.) Other solutions are the
formation of CSA groups and the transformation
of school yards into fruit-and-vegetable gardens.

Planners, community activists and community
organisations are also putting food 'on the table' in
a conceptual sense by recognising and enhancing the
connections that food production and selling have
to many other needs and activities – nutrition, health,
development and use of open space, job training,
employment, economic development and
entrepreneurship. The three founders of People's
Grocery in West Oakland, California – Malaika Edwards,
Vrham Ahmadi and Leander Sellers – recognised just
such connections. Keen to find ways to build economic
empowerment in a very poor, minority community,
they saw food as relating, intrinsically, to everyone,
as a good way to 'start localising our means of
production and what we use', and also answering
a 'huge need for healthy, affordable food'.

In a community of 25,000 residents with only one
grocery store, 36 convenience stores and liquor stores
selling candy, soda, chips and packaged foods, with
very poor public transport, People's Grocery operates
a groceries truck which brings fresh produce and
healthy packaged food and juices at affordable prices
to between four and six stops throughout the
community each day. The organisation partners with
two community gardens and cultivates three of its
own where, given the serious industrial pollutants in
the soil, it grows only in raised beds and works to
rebuild the soil. Each year it hires and trains a small
group of local high-school students who work full-time
in the summer and part-time during the school year.
The students live on a farm for a week and then work
in the community gardens, help run the mobile market,
participate in decisions and take classes in cooking,
nutrition and business.

At School

If families and neighbourhoods are forced to rely long
enough on prepared foods, purchased from fast-food
chains or corner stores, the knowledge of how to cook
fresh food dies out, no longer being passed on from one
generation to the next. At one time, home economics
courses were plentiful and students (traditionally girls)
learned to cook at school as well as at home. Whilst
such courses are rare today, schools that grow fruit
and vegetables in the school yard also include cooking
and meal preparation activities.

The Willard Greening Project at the Willard School
in Berkeley, California, is so popular with students that
between 50 and 100 students choose to work in the
garden during lunchtime. A series of terraced beds,
a garden shed, chicken coop and a sitting area now
occupy the central space of the school, on what used
to be a neglected, asphalt parking lot. Matt Tsang,
formerly a volunteer from Americorps, now leads the
project, which is a formal part of the sixth-grade
curriculum. Every week 150 sixth-graders participate

Top
New Visions Community Garden, East New York Farms, Brooklyn. Marlene Wilks sells vegetables at East New York Farms that she grows here, for her own enjoyment. 'You know one of my biggest pleasures is to come and see my whole bed of okra. It puts me on a high. When I go out and do my gardening, my pressure goes down.'

Bottom
East New York Farms, Brooklyn. On Saturday mornings, from May to November, an empty site next to the elevated subway in this Brooklyn neighbourhood becomes a lively farmers' market. Residents can buy fresh produce and food products from regional farmers and local community gardens, as well as handicrafts and prepared foods. Cooking demonstrations and live concerts are also held at the market.

other and experience a chance to be stewards of the land. The project staff, who are in the garden before school starts and after it ends, are fun to be with: students come to them to talk, to hang out, learning at the same time that a Coke and fried chicken is not the best breakfast to have. Lunchtime, Tsang says, is chaos – some students digging, others weeding, and others tossing a football nearby as the chickens run around.

Not far from Willard is the Edible School Yard at Martin Luther King Jr Middle School, started in 1997 by Alice Waters, founder of the Berkeley restaurant Chez Panisse. With a full acre of cultivated land adjacent to the school, a spacious tool shed storing shovels and rubber boots, and a building for cooking and eating meals, the Edible School Yard benefits from private funding but sponsors the same types of activities as Willard. Under the leadership of David Hawkins, its original manager, the students designed and built the garden in free-form beds in the shape of letters. Classes are held under an oak tree. Given the large size of the garden, good compost is produced, further enriched by manure from a local horse farm. In one bed, the 'three sisters' of Native American culture grow together – corn, beans and squash. Fruit trees of apples, pears, figs, persimmons and plums, guavas and lemons join a wide range of vegetables including pumpkins, squash, artichokes, kohlrabi, garlic, lettuces, chard and kale.

Kelsey Siegel, the current garden supervisor at the Edible School Yard, notes that children are more likely to eat something new if they have grown it themselves: 'In growing the food and eating it, students learn about ecology through observation.' Because cooperation, group decision-making and team-building are required, students 'learn about each other ... It's the conversations out here that are so important.' In the garden, children learn by doing, working side by side with adults, much as apprentices once did. 'Here they are interacting with adults on equal terms and they are contributing.'

In the Neighbourhood
Every Saturday morning, from May to November, a vacant asphalt site next to the elevated subway line in East New York, Brooklyn, is transformed into a lively farmers' market. Produce from local community gardens and three to four family farms in the region, handicrafts, home-made baklava, cooking demonstrations by the Cornell University Coop Extension programme and possibly a mid-morning concert draw about 12,000 customers a season, many Russians, African-Americans and Latinos. At the height of the summer, a queue forms before the market opens. Under one of the white tents, twin sisters Marlene Wilks and Pauline Reid sell Jamaican *galaloo*, mustard greens, collard greens and other vegetables and herbs from the gardens in their yards,

in the gardening/cooking programme. Over the course of a year, students experience all aspects of agriculture – seeding, weeding, harvesting and composting. At the end of each class the students sit down together and eat a snack prepared from the garden produce (possibly cooked greens or fresh carrots, or sweet foods made from amaranth seed and roasted sunflower syrup), participating in an experience that is often absent from their home lives. Students can also take elective courses in the seventh and eighth grades and participate in after-school gardening and cooking activities. Members of those groups have cooked meals for as many as 200 people – for the eighth-grade dinner dance, chow mein for family literacy night and pasta with pasta sauce for family math night.

Tsang finds that the garden provides a different way to learn. Through it, children connect with other things in life, learn to work cooperatively, learn to be sociable with each and from their plots in the nearby New Visions Community Garden.

East New York Farms grew out of an analysis of both the needs and the resources of this Brooklyn neighbourhood. Under an outreach and planning grant from the US Department of Housing and Urban Development, the Pratt Institute Center for Community and Environmental Design discovered 106 community gardens in the area, the highest number of any community in the city. Health is a serious concern, and so is the lack of supermarkets (only three for 68,000 residents).

As with People's Grocery, those who developed the idea of the market realised it would draw upon local resources (gardens, gardening knowledge and available land), would not require capital investment, and could hire, train and pay local youths while also providing fresh produce. With the participation of local community organisations and a variety of grants, the market has been operating since 1998. The intention is to draw enough customers and vendors to become self-sustaining. So far, sales have increased every year from a gross of $900 in 1999 to $80,000 in 2003. As with other farmers' markets which attract low-income customers, its success relies heavily upon the Farmers

Around the world, collapsible white tents, easily set up, folded up and transported, mark full-day or half-day open-air farmers' markets, easily held in a plaza, parking lot, empty site or street closed to traffic. In many cities, markets are also held, every day, in handsome market halls and sheds. Not only are customers and vendors protected from the weather, and not only do the buildings offer a wide array of products and activities, but the architecture and permanence of a market contribute to the character of the area and, possibly, of the entire city.

Market Nutrition Program coupons from the state and federal governments that provide $20 per summer to senior citizens and $24 to families, who receive food stamps for purchase of produce from farmers' markets.

Farmers' markets have sprung up all across the US: between 1994 and 2002, the number increased from 1,775 to 3,137.[2] However, not all of them succeed, and the challenge is even greater in low-income neighbourhoods. The Southland Farmers' Market Association in Los Angeles has reported that 30 per cent of new farmers' markets in California have failed.[3] In its study of public markets, which includes farmers' markets, the Project for Public Spaces notes how important it is for markets in low-income neighbourhoods to draw customers from outside as well as from within the neighbourhood. Parking space, nearby public transit and walkability can all contribute to this.[4]

In the Building and the District

Around the world, collapsible white tents, easily set up, folded up and transported, mark full-day or half-day open-air farmers' markets, easily held in a plaza, parking lot, empty site or street closed to traffic. In many cities, markets are also held, every day, in handsome market halls and sheds. Not only are customers and vendors protected from the weather, and not only do the buildings offer a wide array of products and activities, but the architecture and permanence of a market contribute to the character of the area and, possibly, of the entire city. Some cities have worked hard to preserve such markets – for example, Pike Place Market, which struggled to survive against pressures to redevelop this section of Seattle, and is now such a tourist destination that local residents may find it too crowded for their liking. In addition, many cities are renovating and revitalising market buildings and surrounding areas, or converting existing buildings for market use, as with the Ferry Plaza Farmers' Market in San Francisco.

Findlay Market in Cincinnati, Ohio, is the last of what were once nine public markets in the city. The

Left
Eastern Market attracts thousands of retail and wholesale customers. Some vendors have been selling at the market for 50 years or more. Many of the original structures are still in use. Stores in the district sell speciality items in unpretentious surroundings.

Right
The Eastern Market district of 43 blocks is to undergo a $30 million renovation and reinvestment project, including upgrading and expanding the sheds, improving building facades, making street improvements and organising more year-round events. The first grant of $100,000 was awarded in June 2004.

Notes
1 Kameshwari Pothukuchi and Jerome L Kaufman, 'The food system', Journal of the American Planning Association 66:2, 2000, p 113.
2 USDA Farmers Markets Growth: www.ers.usda.gov. Cited by Alessandro DeGregori, 'Two farmers markets in New Jersey', unpublished research paper, New Jersey Institute of Technology, 2004.
3 Project for Public Spaces, Markets as a Vehicle for Social Integration and Upward Mobility, Project for Public Spaces (New York), 2003.
4 Ibid.
5 Ibid.
6 Theodore Spitzer and Hilary Baum, Public Markets and Community Revitalization, Urban Land Institute and Project for Public Spaces (Washington DC), 1995.
7 For discussions of the food system, see Kameshwari Pothukuchi and Jerome L Kaufman, op cit, pp 113–24, and Kameshwari Pothukuchi and Jerome L Kaufman, 'Placing the food system on the urban agenda', Agriculture and Human Values 16, 1999, pp 213–44.
8 See also the Winter 2004 issue of Progressive Planning: The Magazine of Planners Network, No 158, dedicated to food and planning.

neighbourhood, called 'Over the Rhine', is a low-income, mostly African-American community. The market has survived and was recently renovated despite serious crime problems and loss of local population. It draws vendors from Ohio, Kentucky and Indiana, and customers from all over the city and the suburbs beyond.[5]

Detroit's Eastern Market, the largest wholesale and retail market in the US, is undergoing a $30-million reinvestment and renovation. The five large farmers' sheds, owned and operated by the city, are the centre of a historic market district, containing hundreds of food-related businesses in privately owned buildings. The selling of fresh produce has generated an entire food district of 43 blocks.[6] That Eastern Market has survived and thrived in a city that has undergone as many urban problems as Detroit is truly remarkable, providing evidence of the enduring value of food-related businesses located in close proximity to each other on sites that, for many, are easy to reach. The renovation project includes improving and expanding the sheds, improving facades and streets, and offering more special events.

Food as a System

Once food in the city is recognised not as an independent item nor as a matter of self-indulgent urban lifestyles, but as a dense network of activities and organisations with numerous social, economic and health consequences comprising complex systems, our understanding of urban life and its problems is profoundly improved and a rich series of programmes, policies and physical interventions can be developed and implemented.[7] The cases described here recognise and nurture a wide range of connections, demonstrating the many ways in which food can operate as a social, economic, nutritional, educational and entrepreneurial mechanism, and as a tool for increasing the health of individuals, communities, cities and even regions. Increasing availability and affordability of fresh food becomes both an end in itself and a means of reaching other goals.

Programmes that were born with certain goals have broadened their scope, and organisations with different individual goals find a common ground in food-related projects. In 2000, the New York Greenmarket programme, jointly with other organisations, started the New Farmer Development Project (NFDP) that identifies, educates and supports immigrants with agricultural experience in establishing their own small-scale food-production operations. The project offers the farmer trainees practical education, business and marketing courses, technical assistance and access to farmland. People and organisations dedicated to improving food security work with those who wish to develop local economic initiatives and job-training programmes, as well as organisations that support and advise community gardens. In 2004, the group that sponsors East New York Farms organised a conference on 'Food, Justice and Healthy Families'. And government programmes that seek to preserve farmland recognise the tool of subsidising low-income families to purchase produce from the farms.

Food is beginning to be recognised as a planning issue, not just an agricultural matter.[8] As towns and cities begin to appreciate the value of outdoor farmers' markets, market buildings and market districts, as a service and an amenity for all residents, as well as tourists, and as a means of increasing economic and social vitality downtown, selling food becomes an urban design matter as well. Growing food can also become a concern for urban designers. It is possible to adopt urban design strategies and plans that maintain and strengthen food-growing areas, or that include locations for new ones. Urban agriculture poses a wealth of design opportunities for architects and landscape architects, not just in housing or residential spaces, but next to schools and, perhaps, work places as well. ∆

Tasting the Periphery: Bangkok's Agri- and Aquacultural Fringe

Brian McGrath **and** Danai Thaitakoo **survey the ecosystem of Bangkok, 'an amphibious city' situated on a silted tidal delta. Influenced by Western planning ideas, the major roadways and infrastructure projects constructed since the Second World War remain out of kilter with local conditions. It is as if a consumer society, networked to global media and transport links, has been 'superimposed on a wet rice-cultivating landscape'.**

43

Above
The surface Eastern Ring Road
with its two parallel-frontage
road bridges above major trunk
canals creates covered new
public spaces shaded by a
concrete ceiling that vibrates
with the constant flow of traffic.

The human mouth is a minutely receptive
landscape consisting of folded bumpy surfaces
of papillae tightly embedded with cellular
aggregations called taste buds. Each bud opens
a pore to the watery oral environment, and the
sense of taste is the ability to recognise and
respond to various chemical molecules and ions
dissolved in this mix.[1] Taste evolved to sustain
life by enticing nourishment and detecting
poisons or spoiled food. Yet enjoyable flavours
become ends in themselves, and our mouths
communicate the pleasures of taste through the
social act of language with its rich metaphors
and associations.

The word taste is employed in English as a
noun for a high sensibility in art or culture, but
in Thai, *chim* is used as a verb to allegorically
express a zest for life – the impulse to try or
experience something new or novel. Reconsider,
then, taste as a key metaphor in urban design,
not as a sense of refinement or class, but as an
expression of *élan vital*, the will to encounter
urban life as varied novel sensory experiences.
Attention to taste measures material encounters
between bodies and environments, and connects
our inner and outer worlds. Tasting the city,
therefore, links individual sensation, perception
and impulse with social relations and
environmental awareness. This essay tastes the
periphery of Bangkok as a call for the urban to
be tasted rather than to define urbane taste.[2]

The Bight of Bangkok

Between May and October, a slight shift in atmospheric
currents brings monsoon rains northeast from the
Andaman Sea to Thailand. Seasonal cycles of
precipitation rather than extremes of winter and
summer bring rhythm to life just above the equator,
putting into motion human cycles of planting,
harvesting and migration harmonised with water flows.
Siamese urbanity evolved from intimate association
with climatic, topographic and hydrological conditions.
Upland mountain rainforests release their sacred
mixture through river tributaries converging on wet
rice-cultivating capitals. From 1350, amphibious
Ayutthaya rose to dominate the region from the
confluence of three rivers. An island garden city of
palaces, monasteries, forests, orchards and paddies,
the city retained six months of rain for the following
six dry ones. The fluvial geography was overcoded
by a feudal tributary power system as Ayutthaya was
positioned to receive political tribute from upstream
vassals and lesser kings. Auratic power reflected back
to village hinterlands from the King of Siam, Lord of
the Earth, Forests and Waters, invisible yet all powerful,
within the Inner Court of the Grand Palace.[3]

In 1767, Ayutthaya was destroyed by the Burmese,
and a new capital city was built first at Thonburi and
then moved across the river to Bangkok, downstream
on a sparsely populated plain near the mouth of the
Chao Phraya River. The meandering river forms
numerous oxbows and a network of minor waterways in
the flat delta, creating a distributory as well as tributary

water circulatory system. As a vast, flat water reception and dispersion area, the Chao Phraya Delta is ideally suited for the wet cultivation of rice, yet was inhospitable to human habitation as rainy and dry cycles created either a vast, shallow lake or a parched desert landscape. Yet the lower delta was populated even in the Ayutthaya era, as kings constructed shortcut canals and an inter-river transportation and defence network that became settlement sites. Scattered farming villages extended along watery tentacles, creating an urban/agricultural network centred on the royal city, contained within lush gardens on raised walled and moated islands.[4]

Amphibious Bangkok must be savoured slowly when approached from the river's mouth. Before industrialised prawn-farming, mangrove forests shielded a vast biodiversity of shore birds, crab-eating monkeys, fishing cats, mudskipper fish, sea turtles, dolphins, manatees, otters and a host of fish, molluscs and crustaceans.[5] The city sprawls further upstream amidst the flat, silted tidal delta, unfolding along the meandering course of the river with its countless wandering inlets feeding irrigated orchards and paddies shielded beyond the shady water edges.

Contemporary life in a newly industrialised country follows the less predictable fluctuations of global capital. Thailand's strategic Cold War alliance with the US catapulted the kingdom's economy to a world stage, and as a result new

products, ideas and desires from abroad now mix freely with ancient practices, myths and rites. When rice prices fall, and word of jobs in Bangkok reaches small subsistence agricultural settlements, economic migrations trickle, and then flood, to factories radiating from the capital city. Now, media flows upstream, and television infiltrates nearly every village household in the kingdom. Bangkok broadcasts images and messages much more rapidly and viscerally to the TV screens of the rural majorities than news and laws reached them from the kings of the past, producing more impulsive and less predictable responses.

Cutting through greater Bangkok's densely cultivated fringe are new, monumental multilane expressways speeding human migrations and material distributions. Evident from satellite imagery, this emerging network constitutes an entirely new order: a networked consumer society superimposed on a wet-rice-cultivating landscape. Following neither the web of waterways, nor the radiating ribbons of older canals and roads, these limited access routes represent limited access, hyper movement, just-in-time distribution and high-velocity bypass. Linking these new superhighways is the nearly completed Outer Ring Road, a possible route from which to taste Bangkok's agri- and aquacultural periphery.

Greater Bangkok's new ring road is a circuiting elliptical panorama offering new urban stories and interfaces between the Bight of Bangkok and the outskirts of ancient Ayutthaya. Historically, southeast Asian cities have been oriented around great

Above
The limited-access elevated Southern Ring Road has yet to bridge the Chao Phraya River, and thus offers an extended terrace from which to overlook Bangkok's changing land-cover pattern.

nonperspectival circumambulatory narrative architectural spaces. Bas-reliefs in the ambulatory colonnades of Angkor Wat depict figures churning the great mythological 'sea of milk' – the Siamese version of the Indic *Ramayana* epic unfolds along cloistered murals at Bangkok's royal Temple of the Emerald Buddha.

We conducted our circumambulatory excursion on the Outer Ring Road in August, at the beginning of the monsoon rains that coincide with the start of Buddhist Lent. Millions of Thais performed the ritual *vientien*, circuiting the sacred *chedi* at their local temples three times under the full moon while we circuited the ring twice in our van. Our tour began near the site of the new Suwannabhumi Airport, named for the golden age of southeast Asian civilisation before European colonisation. The airport will reterritorialise the region, reconnecting ancient capitals divided by the Cold War – Pagan in Myanmar, Luang Prabang in Laos and Siem Reap in Cambodia – resituating Bangkok's agri- and aquacultural fringe within tourist circuits of southeast Asia.

Stops on the Ring Road
While Bangkok's Outer Ring Road rationalises regional truck and auto transportation, and provides access to an array of peripheral factories, shopping centres and housing estates, it also provides new perceptions and experiences of the city as it passes marginalised canal-based agri- and aquacultural landscapes. Bangkok's ring cobbles together three highway types: the newly completed limited-access surface Eastern

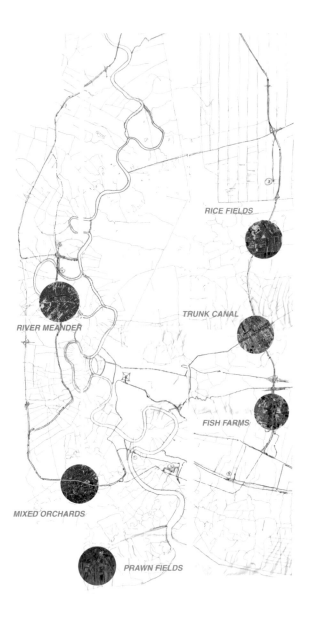

RICE FIELDS

TRUNK CANAL

RIVER MEANDER

FISH FARMS

MIXED ORCHARDS

PRAWN FIELDS

Right
Stops along the Outer Ring Road include fish farms, found public space under the highway along west bank meanders, and east bank trunk canals, rice fields, mixed orchards and prawn fields.

Below
The Bung Tong Fishing Hut serves freshwater-pond fish immediately adjacent to the Outer Ring Road, but is only accessible via an elaborate detour off the frontage road and through an industrial estate and a golf-course residential development.

Ring; the already urbanised unlimited-access surface Western Ring; and the incomplete limited-access elevated Southern Ring. The three sections situate relationships of traffic to land differently, and present to the high-speed traveller a varied patchwork of geomorphic and hydrological properties shaped by historical human interventions.

The Outer Ring passes freshwater fish ponds in the low-lying area above the dyked eastern industrial seaboard, the vast irrigated rice fields of Rangsit to the northeast, and poldered mixed-fruit orchards that cling to the west bank's meandering river banks, and skirts north of the western seaboard's vast coastal prawn fields. From satellite imagery, the fish,

rice, fruit and prawn production areas are distinct and homogeneous, but field examination on the ground reveals a surprisingly heterogeneous pattern with many local disturbances.

The East Bank: Fish Farms, Wet Rice Cultivation and Subdivisions

Driving counterclockwise from the surface Eastern Ring, we initially cross the perennial wet zone directly east of central Bangkok. This low-lying inland area comprises freshwater streams, swamps and fish-farming ponds, and the enormous construction site of Bangkok's new airport. Surviving fish farms near the highway have added restaurants and fishing pavilions along ponds to supplement their income. However, this section of the highway has limited access and is

barricaded behind a double embankment, large drainage gulley and a fenced frontage road. A hungry traveller or weekend fisherman can find access to these facilities only by taking elaborate detours and U-turns through industrial estates and golf-course communities.

To the north is Minburi, the site of Lucien Hanks' landmark human-ecosystem study of the Ban Chan rice-growing community. Hanks carefully documented extended-family households who responded to changing market and technological conditions through an intricate feedback system, moving from shifting, to broadcasting and, finally, to transplanting rice during Thailand's first period of modernisation. Hanks' study demonstrated how village-level decisions affected environmental change in concert with shifting market trends.[6] The present landscape is much more fragmented and heterogeneous, with many methods of cultivation and income-producing activities competing, and various stages of planting, growth and harvesting coexisting. Historical evolution and seasonal rhythms have collapsed into a mixed-time image of lapsed land-use fragmentation and superposition.

The endless flat plane of Rangsit consists of 200,000 hectares with no large rivers or topographic relief. In the 1890s, Dutch hydrologist Homan van der Heide, the first director-general of Siam Land, Canals and Irrigation Co, rationally planned the diversion of water through 20 straight north–south canals, 30 to 40 kilometres long and spaced at 2 kilometres, with smaller numbered irrigation canals repeated at 1-kilometre intervals. Large areas were opened up for habitation as feeder canals assured a steady water supply for newly developed paddy fields. In the early 20th century, the Bangkok periphery became the primary rice bowl for the region, and the kingdom's primary economic base. With global food shortages following the Second World War, World Bank loans allowed the completion of van der Heide's plan of a modern irrigation system, resulting in a human-controlled water system where growing cycles could be in sync with markets rather than seasonal precipitation.[7]

Now, however, the emerald-green carpet of

Rangsit's fields extends in narrow rows chequered with a grey pattern of new housing and factory estates. Developers have planted these crowded single-family homes and factories in dense rows on the kingdom's most fertile soil. Along Canal Road 3, fishing nets are suspended over the waterway, and narrow wooden pedestrian bridges cross to rice-farming villages hidden behind jungle-like vegetation. A few kilometres down the road, a giant helium balloon marks the entrance to a new housing estate perpendicular to the canal. A security guard stiffly salutes outside a gated estate raised above, and walled from, the surrounding paddies. Inside, a faux New-England-common green lawn is lined with concrete colonial homes with terracotta roofs in four varieties. crowded together within the former rice plot.

The West Bank: Crossing the Meanders – Orchards, Gardens and Gated Communities

The older, unlimited-access Western Ring Road is already urbanised – an endless strip of malls, factories and shops. The newly constructed middle ring, Ratchapruek Road, is a better route from which to examine the thickly vegetated orchards along the river meanders. This area is a poldered flood-control reservoir, where excess water from the city centre is discharged. A west bank orchard and vegetable garden consists of a corduroy pattern of rows of small dredged canals alternating with built-up mounds. The layered tree canopy of a deltaic mixed orchard consists of spindly betel nut and sugar palms at the highest level, blocking little sunlight from the next layer of coconut palm, durian, mango, pomelo, jackfruit, rose apple, star fruit, mangosteen, guava, rambutan, rose apple, banana trees and orange saplings. The lowest layer consists of vegetables or herbs, benefiting from the filtering of the

strong tropical sun. However, all over the west bank, this cool, aromatic and verdant mix, the green lung of greater Bangkok, is rapidly being replaced by upmarket gated housing estates taking advantage of the attraction of a lush green area now minutes away from the centre of the city.

The Southern Ring: Orchards, Prawn Fields and Factories

The Southern Ring is a long viaduct raised above the perennial wet zone north of the coastal prawn fields on the west bank. There is no access to the farms below, but traffic is light enough for truckers to pull off and have a snack from food vendors overlooking the fields. Coconut palms still line the major supply canals, but much land is uncultivated, and unpicked coconuts clog the canals. Labour-intensive fruit production has declined and farmers widen irrigation ditches below in order to farm fish inside the orchard canals. The type of fish varies depending on market demands and water quality, and provides a temporary source of income on land awaiting redevelopment.

The Chao Phraya has yet to be bridged by the ring road to the south, and the eastern connection of the Southern Ring Road is still on the drawing board. Exploring the right of way of the new highway, we listen to the stories of several residents. Most orchards have been abandoned for decades, awaiting a highway planned almost 30 years ago. One farmer is growing orchids, not dependent on a clean water supply. He has a large banner over the canal

telling neighbours not to accept the government's minimal land-purchase offer. Although on this rainy-season day the canal water is flowing clean and fresh following a downpour, farmers assure us that the canals often turn black when nearby factories discharge waste water directly into supply canals.

Conclusion: Slow Food on a Fast Road

Despite the verdant image from remote sensing, the periphery of Bangkok leaves the oily and bitter aftertaste of environmental degradation and rampant land speculation amid the struggles of small farmers. How does a hastily growing city manage such a vast and sensitive territory? Bangkok's periphery has benefited little from 50 years of Western master-planning advice. The government recently built southeast Asia's largest water-treatment plant financed by large international loans, yet it remains unconnected to industrial and residential developments. The Outer Ring Road is conceived at the scale and ambition of Abercrombie's 1948 Green Belt Plan for London, but Bangkok is not a postwar bombed-out capital city of a shrinking empire.[8] A similar sprawl-containment strategy is not possible in this rapidly developing metropolis already marked by a vastly dispersed industrial and residential fringe, where orchard- and rice-farmers struggle behind car-manufacturing plants and chains of suppliers, or in the path of voracious housing development.

Instead, localised strategies must be deployed on the ground. The ecological theory of patch dynamics reflects a paradigm shift in the understanding of socio-natural urban interrelationships, and better equips us to tackle the design challenges of greater Bangkok's shifting mosaic of farm, factory and housing development strung together by new expressways.

Right
Ban Rai Café franchises sit on
the edge of the modern highway
and petrol station landfill,
overlooking rice paddies.
Seducing with a sip of coffee,
Ban Rai captures and engages
its customers within this
transitional ecology between
two cultures and two eras,
whilst straddling two
landscapes: one a shady wet
vegetated oasis, the other a
heat-radiating dry highway.

Below
Where the flyover of
Ratchapruek Road soars across
the old course of the Chao
Phraya River, a new public
beach has formed over Khlong
Bangkok Noi.

Notes
1 Tim Jacob, 'The Physiology of
Taste'. See www.cf.ac.uk/biosi/
staff/jacob/teaching/sensory/ta
ste.html.
2 Personal conversation with
Jean Gardner, Parsons School
of Design.
3 Thongchai Winichakul, *Siam
Mapped: A History of the Geo-
Body of a Nation*, University of
Hawaii Press (Honolulu), 1997.
4 Yoshikazu Takaya, *Agricultural
Development of a Tropical
Delta: A Study of the Chao
Phraya Delta*, University of
Hawaii Press (Honolulu), 1987.
5 TED Case Studies, 'Thai
Shrimp Farming'. See
www.american.edu/TED/
THAISHMP.HTM.

6 Lucien Hanks, *Rice and Man*, Aldine Publishing Co (Chicago), 1972.
7 Takaya, op cit.
8 Personal conversation with Grahame Shane, Columbia University.
9 Steward Pickett, lecture at Columbia University, Graduate School of Architecture, Planning and Preservation, 11 October 2004.
10 Paul Ryan of Newschool University has developed video work based on a similar notion of a 'relational circuit'.
11 The acquisition of ASTER data was supported by a research project, 'Investigation of Rapid Urbanization Processes Using ASTER, MODIS, and Landsat Data', by Dr Philip Christensen, Principal Investigator, NASA Grant number: EOS/03-0000-0502. The ASTER data are distributed by the Land Processes Distributed Active Archive Center (LP DAAC) located at the US Geological Survey's EROS Data Center (http://LPDAAC.usgs.gov).

Acknowledgement
The authors would like to thank the Thailand Research Fund, International START Secretariat, and the research project 'Investigation of Rapid Urbanization Processes Using ASTER, MODIS, and Landsat Data' for their partial support for this article.

For ecologist Steward Pickett, ecosystem patch dynamics can provide meaning, models and metaphors for architects and planners. According to patch dynamic theory, ecologies are open, heterogeneous, indeterminate systems where disturbance and outside forces can alter resources and environmental regulators. Conventional notions of nature consisting of closed systems in ecological balance or equilibrium are erroneous.[9] A patch dynamic approach to design would direct human-ecosystem monitoring, management and design of air, water and waste flows locally, on site, with information flowing up to government officials and policy makers.[11]

The daily acts of eating, breathing and drinking bring awareness to the sensory aspects of existence and give insight towards comprehending the city as an ecosystem. Taste and sensual pleasure are design tools that take into account the biophysical and sociocultural life-support conditions of a site. The 19th-century industrial city's aqueducts and parks were not just engineering infrastructures, but powerful symbols of hope for a healthy and hygienic metropolis. As a detour from master-planning, this essay's excursion along Bangkok's new Outer Ring Road contemplates how a patch

dynamic approach would culturally revalue pockets of the city's agri- and aquacultural fringe in order to provide breathing space, temperature moderation, water-quality maintenance and new perspectives among peripheral expressways, shopping malls, and industrial and housing estates.

Like in ancient Siam, watersheds structure a patch dynamic ecosystem approach, but unlike the feudal kingship, suggest the possibilities of a bottom-up approach for emerging democracies. In recognising patchy rather than centralised urban development, localised air-, water- and food-quality management could be strung among the underutilised open spaces concentrated on the orchard meanders and the long, ancient irrigation canals, made visible and publicly accessible from the ring road. Physical connections provide feedback loops between farmers, consumers and policy-makers. Bangkok's Outer Ring Road could become an attentive circuit,[10] connecting modern travel patterns with environmental monitoring. This is not just an engineering solution towards sustainability, but the recognition of a patchy new symbolic realm as well as a sensual and seductive new cultural space. Here, the urban populace might taste the city periphery as an ecosystem along highway detours and rest stops: slow food on a fast road would engage people in bioregional knowledge as part of daily life.[11] Δ

Urban Agriculture:
Small, Medium, Large

Could urban agriculture be the next design revolution? **Gil Doron** explains how horticulture, a subject that has until now remained remote from the concerns of contemporary architects, is ripe with potential, bringing with it many ecological, economic and social benefits for the city dweller. He also points out that at all levels, whether at the scale of window boxes, balconies or roof gardens, or on the scale of full-blown farms, vegetation and agriculture exist in most cities in the world right underneath our noses.[1]

When everyone was asked to propose ideas for improving our inner-city block at a recent tenants meeting, I suggested transforming the front lawn and roof into food-producing gardens. The idea first came to me when I saw a Chinese couple trespassing on our lawn to pick pears from a tree I didn't think yielded any edible fruits. Apparently, these pears can be cooked and made into jam. My proposal was to divide the front lawn into allotments of about 10 metres by 30 metres. Each flat would maintain its own allotment where residents could grow vegetables, hire the local gardener to grow vegetables for them, maintain a lawn or rent their allotments to other residents. The roof top would also be used for growing herbs and vegetables in large containers. To my surprise, a few elderly tenants responded immediately with the question: 'Is there going to be a war?'

During the two world wars, urban agriculture flourished in England's cities. The real threat of starvation posed by blockades prompted campaigns to increase indigenous food output, much of it from urban agriculture. During the First World War, the number of allotments roughly tripled from around 450,000 to 1.5 million. At the outbreak of the Second World War, the UK's minister of agriculture launched the 'Dig for Victory' campaign, as part of which more than half of all manual workers produced food from either an allotment or their gardens. However, after the war and throughout the 1950s and 1960s, a great deal of food-growing land was returned to its original prewar uses or lost to new development. The combined effect of the new welfare state, effectively full employment and increasing prosperity meant that people no longer saw a need to grow their own food.

Reasons for Urban Agriculture

Today, economic hardship is the main reason why urban agriculture is so common in cities in developing countries. Across Chinese cities, 85 per cent of vegetables consumed by residents are produced within those cities, and Shanghai and Beijing are fully self-sufficient in vegetables (Hough, 1995).[2] In other Asian and Latin American cities, between 10 per cent and 30 per cent of the fruit and vegetables consumed is produced within the city's limits. The greatest amount of urban farming can be found in Havana, where it is promoted and sometimes financed by the state: for example, there are 20,000 small orchards and plots on a total of 2,770 hectares. Most, if not all, of the food production in the capital is organic.[3]

Urban agriculture holds economic benefits for developed countries as well. The US government's urban gardening programme estimates that a $1 investment in food-growing projects yields $6 of produce. Urban agriculture on a small scale can complete the food basket for the poorer population in Western cities and generate jobs in food growing, processing and marketing. A number of developed and relatively affluent countries and cities understand these benefits: for example, Hong Kong urban agriculture meets 45 per cent of local demand for vegetables, and Singapore is relatively self-sufficient in pork, poultry and eggs, and grows 25 per cent of all the vegetables consumed by its population.[4] Most surprisingly, according to the US Department of Agriculture, a third of the country's agricultural output comes from urban/metropolitan areas.

The environmental benefits are as much an incentive for growing food in cities as the economic ones. The current global food economy is heavily reliant upon nonrenewable resources (gas and land) and generates a large amount of waste. Growing food in the city shortens the distance between producer and consumer, thus cutting energy consumption considerably. It was suggested recently that if food in the UK were produced organically, consumed locally, and only when in season, the level of carbon dioxide emissions would be reduced by 22 per cent. This reduction is twice the amount the UK has committed to under the Kyoto Protocol. Urban agriculture also brings some reduction in the demand for land resources since it decreases the need for

landfills for waste through the use of composting and less packaging.

Involvement in growing food is a healthy occupation and a popular way of relieving stress. More formal horticultural therapy has helped those suffering from mental health problems, and is also used in rehabilitating homeless people with drug- and alcohol-abuse problems.

Growing food in a communal way, in community gardens and city farms, breaks down barriers between people with regard to differences in age, ethnicity, class and gender, stimulates a sense of 'ownership' of, and pride in, the local environment, and galvanises people to cooperate on other issues of social concern. City farms and community gardens also have educational value, with some schools incorporating food growing into the teaching of science, geography, maths and environmental education.

20th-Century Architecture

Urban food-growing in general, and allotments in particular, featured prominently in Ebenezer Howard's *Garden Cities of Tomorrow*, first published in 1902.[5] In each city, five-sixths of the area was devoted to food production. Residential space was to be divided into generous plots of 20 feet by 130 feet, which Howard envisaged would be sufficient to feed a family of at least five people. In addition, allotments ringed the settlement peripheries.

Critically building on Howard's ideas, Le Corbusier promoted pre-urban and urban agriculture on a large scale in his 'Contemporary City' proposal expounded in *The City of Tomorrow and its Planning*, first published in 1924.[6] In his 'Contemporary City' plans, Le Corbusier designed three types of sites where food could be grown: in unmediated proximity to the city, in the 'protected zones', he envisaged large-scale agricultural fields; for detached suburban homes, he included large kitchen gardens which took up more than a third of the plot (over 400 square yards); and in his most detailed model for an urban setting – the cellular or honeycomb-type neighbourhood – he combined the kitchen gardens of each flat into one field of allotments, almost 10 acres in size. In this plan, he indicated how the growing of food would be managed:

> There would be a farmer in charge of every 100 such plots and intensive cultivation would be employed. The farmer undertakes all the heavy work. The inhabitant comes back from

his factory or office, and with the renewed strength given him by his games, starts to work on his garden. His plot, cultivated in a standardized and scientific way, feeds him for the greater part of the year. There are storehouses on the borders of each group of plots in which he can store his produce for the winter.[7]

Pre-urban agriculture on a large scale was also introduced by Frank Lloyd Wright in *The Living City*.[8] Wright's vision of the 'living city' could best be summarised as integrating agriculture into dispersed suburban settlements, creating a new landscape. As an idea it transgresses the distinction between urban and suburban, and also helps to articulate a vision of a city driven by ecological intensification, where food growing stands equal to traditional development in the built environment.

The Facade: Windowsills, Balconies and Roof Tops

Urban agriculture, because of its various scales and locations, can be the subject of all design professions – from landscape and urban design, to building and interior design, and even product design. At its smallest scale, food is being grown on windowsills and balconies. Currently there are no statistics showing the number of people in the UK or Europe growing herbs and vegetables in this way. However, the fact that all the major supermarket chains sell herbs growing in pots says something about the demand for this product. It is true that almost any windowsill or balcony can contain a few pots for such growing activities, but windowsills and large balconies purpose-built for agricultural uses can be a selling point of such buildings, and contribute to the promotion of urban agriculture on a small scale. Such design intervention is demonstrated in a new Bed Zed project in Brighton. Another, more radical, proposal is Bohn & Viljoen Architects' green facade for a project in the Shoreditch area of London.

If vertical landscaping on apartment blocks is still a rare phenomenon, roof gardens have become ever more popular, especially in cities where land values and density are high. They are common in the US, Japan and Europe, especially in Switzerland and Germany, where there are planning requirements to install them.[9] Food production is possible on an intensive green roof where the soil is deep enough. Such roofs can hold vegetables and even trees, but are costly at around £150 per square metre, and in residential blocks and private houses it is more usual to see people growing vegetables and herbs in large boxes and pots. Either way, community roof gardens, or simply growing food on balconies, can bring neighbours together and generate a new urban and social space, as shown in a charming project by John Puttick, a Bartlett graduate, who won a RIBA silver medal for his proposal.

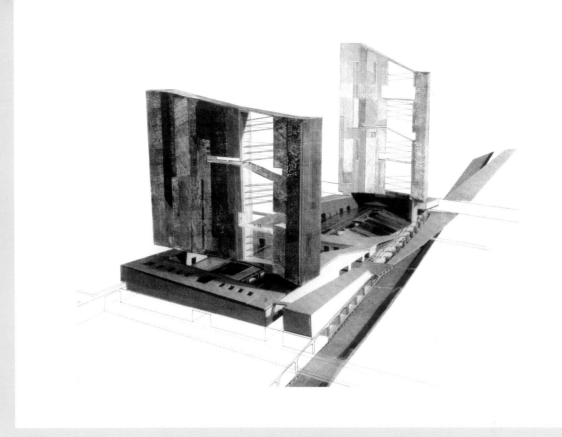

Top

Bohn & Viljoen Architects, proposal for high-density urban agriculture, Shoreditch, East London (in *Continuous Productive Urban Landscapes (CPULS): Designing Urban Agriculture for Sustainable Cities*, Architectural Press, 2005)

A vertical landscape can be productive. In addition to the growing of food, other advantages of the project include saving energy, buffering noise, filtering the air and increased privacy. The aesthetic value of a green facade is also important, changing in colour, density and opacity with the passing of the seasons.

Right

John Puttick, The Land of Scattered Seeds, Graz, Austria, 2003

The project shows how growing food in a dense inner-city block can generate an environmental, social and economic chain reaction. It visualises how two brothers, living in a downtown street in Graz, converted their environment over time (the windowsill, balconies and roof) into a patchwork of farms, vineyards and gardens, which resulted in increased interaction and exchange with their neighbours.

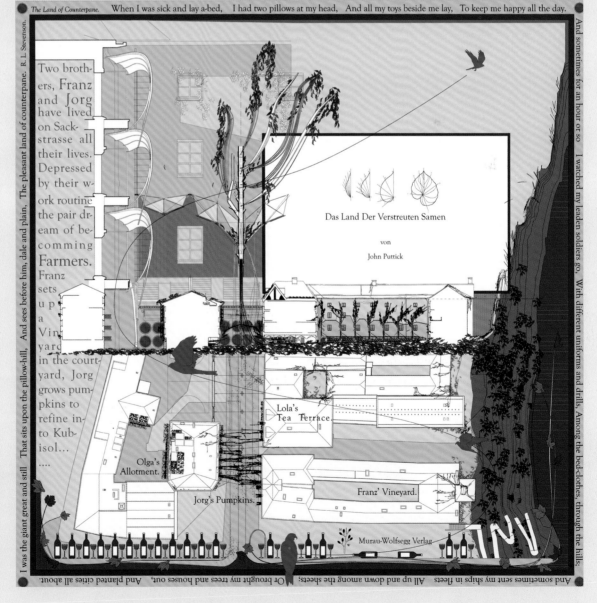

Top
Vauxhall City Farm, London
Set against the background of the MI5 Building in London, Vauxhall City Farm is built on a space that was left over, after planning, at the edge of a churchyard and a park. It offers recreational and educational opportunities for different groups and individuals, with a wide variety of farm animals, an ecology area and a herb garden.

Right
Vauxhall Community Garden, London
The garden adjacent to Vauxhall City Farm is a very modest one, but the demand for land for farming (community gardens or private allotments) is on the rise, with waiting times for allotments in some London boroughs anything up to a year. Overall, each year the city farms and community gardens attract around 650,000 visitors.

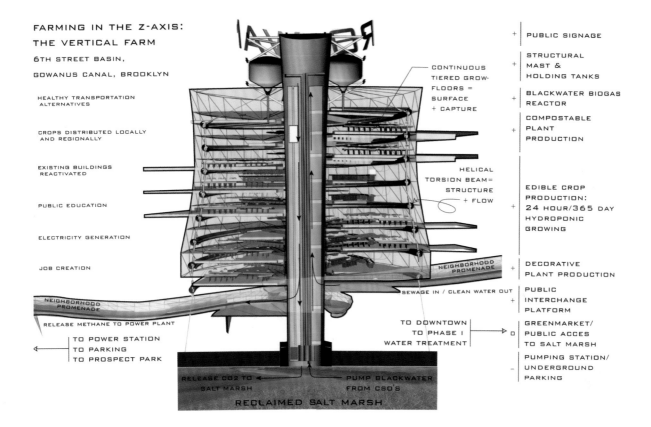

FARMING IN THE Z-AXIS:
THE VERTICAL FARM
6TH STREET BASIN,
GOWANUS CANAL, BROOKLYN

HEALTHY TRANSPORTATION
ALTERNATIVES

CROPS DISTRIBUTED LOCALLY
AND REGIONALLY

EXISTING BUILDINGS
REACTIVATED

PUBLIC EDUCATION

ELECTRICITY GENERATION

JOB CREATION

NEIGHBORHOOD
PROMENADE

RELEASE METHANE TO POWER PLANT

TO POWER STATION
TO PARKING
TO PROSPECT PARK

RELEASE CO2 TO
SALT MARSH

PUMP BLACKWATER
FROM CSO'S

RECLAIMED SALT MARSH

CONTINUOUS
TIERED GROW-
FLOORS =
SURFACE
+ CAPTURE

HELICAL
TORSION BEAM =
STRUCTURE
+ FLOW

NEIGHBORHOOD PROMENADE

SEWAGE IN / CLEAN WATER OUT

TO DOWNTOWN
TO PHASE I
WATER TREATMENT

+ PUBLIC SIGNAGE

+ STRUCTURAL
MAST &
HOLDING TANKS

+ BLACKWATER BIOGAS
REACTOR

+ COMPOSTABLE
PLANT
PRODUCTION

+ EDIBLE CROP
PRODUCTION:
24 HOUR/365 DAY
HYDROPONIC
GROWING

+ DECORATIVE
PLANT PRODUCTION

PUBLIC
INTERCHANGE
PLATFORM

□ GREENMARKET/
PUBLIC ACCES
TO SALT MARSH

— PUMPING STATION/
UNDERGROUND
PARKING

Above
The Vertical Farm, Columbia University, New York, 2004
The farm project is a model for a self-sustaining multistorey urban-agriculture building that could be located in any city centre. It could be used for growing virtually anything, for example, herbs, or for farming animals. Protected from the weather, many crops could be grown all year round. The farm can meet the food demands of a small- to medium-sized city.

The Ground: Allotments, Community Gardens and City Farms

The most common, and by far the largest-scale agriculture in cities takes place on allotments, in community gardens and in city farms. In England, allotments were originally small plots held by agricultural labourers, introduced in the 17th century to compensate such labourers for the private enclosure by rich landlords of common land previously available to all for grazing and cultivation. As the Industrial Revolution drew the rural poor to urban areas, allotments became urban phenomena and were used as a source of money and food. Since 1908, urban allotment provision by the municipal authorities has become mandatory. Though there was a significant drop in the use of allotments after the Second World War, since the early 1970s demand for them has increased.

Alongside this revival, other forms of urban food-growing in the UK, Europe and North America have developed, notably the city farm and community garden movements. The main reasons for this include the growth in environmental ethics and alternative lifestyles, as well as notions of self-sufficiency. While the city farm is a more European phenomenon, and the community garden traditionally a North American one, unlike the allotment both are cultivated and operated as a communal initiative. As such, food production is secondary to their educational and community-bonding roles.

Many community gardens and city farms had been empty sites that were squatted in as an act of self-help and community regeneration and, with the upturn in the economy in cities such as New York, some of them were lost to 'redevelopment'. Nonetheless, community gardens and city farms have become an important part of cities like London and New York: London's city farms and community gardens attract some 650,000 people each year, and in tourist guides to Manhattan, the Lower East Side community garden is one of the most highly recommended places to visit.[10]

Though city farms and community gardens do not offer much flexibility for design intervention, they can be used as sites for design experiments in urban agriculture, especially in the areas of roof gardening, vertical farming and new technologies, ideas currently being discussed by the European Federation of City Farmers.[11]

The Tower and the Continuous Landscape

Vertical farming would need to be introduced if urban agriculture were to become the main supplier of food in cities. With a few exceptions, cities all around the globe are getting denser and urbanisation, even in dispersed forms, will not leave much available land for conventional farming in or outside the city. It is unlikely that agriculture could compete successfully with other usages, like housing, offices or even recreational open spaces.

Based on these assumptions, Professor Dickson Despommier from the Department of Environmental Health Sciences at Columbia University, in collaboration with the Urban Design Programme, headed by Professor Richard Plunz, have developed the Vertical Farm project. The idea was originally developed to sustain the nutritional needs of 50,000 people in New

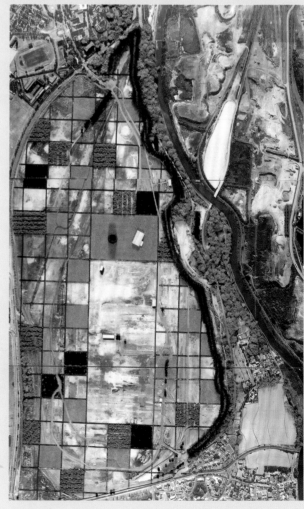

York City. The model consists of a 48-storey
building, either 90,000 square feet or 250,000
square feet. The crops would be cultivated by a
hydroponics system based on the nutrient film
technique, which is the most intensive crop-
production method currently in use. The farm
would have zero net emissions, and derive its
energy from methane gas collected from the
farm waste as well as the waste of restaurants
in the area. It would also be a closed loop, where
water would be 100 per cent recycled. The
Vertical Farm is currently looking for a private
or corporate entrepreneur to finance the second
phase of the project and begin feasibility trials.

Pig City, by MVRDV, grew out of a similar
analysis of the insufficiency of farmland and the
problem of disease and energy waste. It would
meet the demand for pork in the Netherlands
as well as in countries importing products from
Holland. Whether or not it is a real design
proposal, the project cleverly addresses the
issue of meat consumption and farming, and is
part of a series of other real, or theoretical,
designs by the group, such as the Expo project,
which address the issues of densification,
compactisation and land-use maximisation
so relevant to urban agriculture.

The most cohesive vision for urban
agriculture was presented recently in the book
CPULs *Continuous Productive Urban Landscapes:
Designing Urban Agriculture for Sustainable*

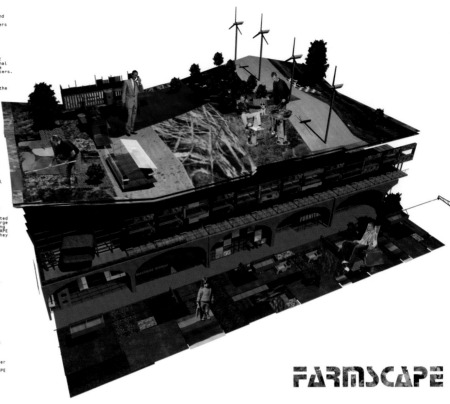

FARMSCAPE

Right

Justin Bridgland, Mark Taylor and Andrew Wood, Bishopsgate Goodsyard, East London, 2003
The proposed programme, by these graduate diploma students in architecture and cultural studies at the Oxford School of Architecture, is to preserve the existing railway arches, inject commercial uses into them and build a new layer on top. One layer will be for housing, on top of which an agricultural field will be laid out. The field is subdivided into strips, each belonging to an apartment below. The crops relate to the imposed topography and are chosen for their aesthetic qualities as much as their nutritional value. The project, like the CPUL, connects large-scale urban design (stretching along several kilometres of the disused railway line) and the production of food.

Notes
1 Unless mentioned otherwise, the three main sources of information for this article were Andre Viljoen (ed), *CPULs Continuous Productive Urban Landscapes (CPULs): Designing Urban Agriculture for Sustainable Cities*, Architectural Press (London), 2005; and Tata Gammett, 'City Harvest Report' for Sustain: The Alliance for Better Food and Farming, 1999 (see www.sustainweb.org/urban_index.asp and various studies published on www.cityfarmer.org/notes.
2 M Hough, 'Cities and Natural Process', in Viljoen, op cit.
3 *New Agriculturist* online magazine (www.new-agri.co.uk).
4 Gammett, op cit.
5 Ebenezer Howard, Garden Cities of To-Morrow (London, 1902). Reprinted, edited with a preface by FJ Osborn and an introductory essay by Lewis Mumford, Faber and Faber (London), 1946, pp 123–47.
6 Le Corbusier, *The City of Tomorrow and Its Planning*, trans from *Urbanism*, with an introduction by Fredrick Etchells, Dover Publications (New York), 1987.
7 Ibid, p 206.
8 Frank Lloyd Wright, *The Living City*, Meridian Books, 1970.
9 Green Roof Report, British Council for Offices, 2003.
10 www.greenthumbnyc.org).
11 See http://efcf.vgc.be.

Cities, edited by Andre Viljoen. CPULs are coherently planned and designed continuous landscapes (a network of open green spaces) that are environmentally and economically productive. For example, a CPUL provides food from urban agriculture, pollution absorption, the cooling effect of trees and increased biodiversity from wildlife corridors. What is appealing about this concept is its introduction of urban design to the issue of urban agriculture. It is a good example of how architectural investigation into a subject that initially seems very remote from design can reframe the subject itself, and open a new field for architectural involvement.

As with the other projects mentioned above, the CPUL aims at cutting carbon dioxide emissions and reducing the distance between the site of production and consumption. At the same time it disperses the spatial and environmental qualities of green sites all over the city. In addition to transforming parts of parks, wastelands, lawns and roofs into a productive landscape, the CPUL concept calls for the introduction of large-scale agricultural fields into the city or city edges, for example on brownfield sites or car parks. Ideally, where possible, fields surrounding existing supermarkets would be created so that food could be sold directly on site. CPUL concepts are demonstrated in Dominique Perrault's design for Caen; and another proposal that uses landscape to invigorate urban life, to produce food locally and to create an exciting landscape, is the City Farm design proposal for Bishopsgate Goodsyard in east London.

Most of the design proposals mentioned above are small-scale interventions, and it took some time to find them at all. Current larger-scale initiatives, such as the Vertical Farm and Pig City, are in their experimental stages. Apparently, the 800 million people who are currently engaged in urban agriculture worldwide, among them 200 million on a commercial basis, manage to flourish without help from architects. However, the results of architectural intervention could make urban agriculture a significant part of every city. It could be the next urban revolution to change the face of our cities. The economic, social and environmental benefits of urban agriculture indeed justify one. ∆

The City as Dining Room:

BIG

Dining in Hong Kong

SIGN

In Hong Kong, open-air eateries that advertise their appetising menus on big signs are the most common informal setting for consuming delicious food with friends and family. **Jeffrey W Cody** and **Mary C Day** seek out these 'big-sign' eating places in the smallest alleyways as well as in the province's fresh-food markets and, perhaps most suprisingly, in the midst of its postwar housing estates.

In Hong Kong, outdoor eateries survive and often
flourish in the guise of unpolished *daipaidongs*
(literally, 'big licence stalls' or 'big-sign places').
'Big signs' – eye-catching placards posting the
day's special dishes – function as menus to
entice customers. Traditionally sprouting up
adjacent to open markets, *daipaidongs* now
pepper many urban neighbourhoods and
sometimes even grace newer malls, albeit in
more antiseptic versions of their former selves.

Big-sign places in what is now called the
Chinese 'Special Administrative Region' of Hong
Kong are open dining rooms that lay bare the
raw thrill that most Hong Kong residents show
in socialising while eating a wide assortment of
food, from delicate Cantonese cuisine (such as
stir-fried jumbo shrimp coated with duck-egg
yolk) to more common fare (such as fish balls
served over a bowl of hot noodles). The culinary
variety of *daipaidongs* always satisfies those who
patronise the casual tables of any big-sign place,
where dishes advertised on such signs often
eliminate the need for individual menus.

Hong Kong's *daipaidongs* are compressed, distant cousins of a wide variety of street-food places which historically have thrived in Chinese cities. As these cities are today transforming themselves into streamlined, more globalised metropolises, they (like Hong Kong) are increasingly erasing the particular food stall in favour of the more sanitised general franchise.

Above
One type of *daipaidong* is relatively diminutive. These open-air cooking stalls are often found in back alleys. Sitting at fold-up tables on plastic stools, patrons fill up on food reminiscent of home cooking. Some stalls operate only during the day (when workers congregate for lunch), while others come alive at night.

Right
A second kind of *daipaidong* expands and contracts in size according to the time of day and the number of customers. More tables can be added at a moment's notice, or the dining operation can be folded up into a cocoon.

In addition to Hong Kongers' pervasive and, seemingly, inherent enjoyment of food, the city's residential density and humid climate have also contributed to the creation and perpetuation of the *daipaidong* as a dynamic place where food is shared in the open.

Outdoor dining is the rule from one end of Asia to the other. The tendency to dine in the open air can be seen from Asia's link to Europe in Istanbul, where people gather to eat freshly fried fish from boats along the Bosporus, to Malaysia where hawkers peddle their aromatic concoctions from small burners pulled from the backs of motorcycles. Across central Asia, hungry folk are tempted to eat salty and spicy shashlik cooked on handmade barbecues that scent the air with wood-smoked meat. And Uighur men in western China – descendants of Turkic nomads who ventured east centuries ago – squat on a kerb, slurping peanut-flavoured noodles from a bowl. Hong Kong's *daipaidongs*, then, are but one traditional answer (found in many variants throughout Asia) to a strongly felt need for outdoor spaces in which to dine with family and friends.

The *daipaidongs* are compressed, distant cousins of a wide variety of street-food places which historically have thrived in Chinese cities. As these cities are today transforming themselves into streamlined, more globalised metropolises, they (like Hong Kong) are increasingly erasing the particular food stall in favour of the more sanitised general franchise. However, throughout China, one can still find the antecedents of Hong Kong's *daipaidongs*: open-air clusters of tables within the orbit of fiery woks, or even table-less places where hungry patrons consume their favourite snacks as they make their way from one urban activity to another. Street markets and fresh food have been mainstays of Chinese urban culture since time immemorial and, despite the myriad political and social changes that have characterised Chinese life for centuries, eating delicious food with friends and family has remained of cardinal importance. Hence, dining in the courtyards of traditional housing complexes is common throughout Chinese history.

So, too, in Hong Kong; yet, because of its colonial history (dominated by the British from 1842 to 1997), Hong Kong developed particular, and often culturally hybrid variations of such eating places. These included higher-end dining palaces for the richer classes (where prostitution sometimes merged with eating and drinking) as well as teahouses and dumpling stalls (where less wealthy patrons socialised whilst eating). The big-sign place became a variant of the sit-down restaurant and the outdoor stall, in part because the rules mandated by the colonial authorities (for example, the need to provide toilets in eating places) also created incentives for avoiding those rules (by driving dining outdoors, for example). The typology of the *daipaidong* is richly varied, but in general it manifests itself in three

main versions: back-alley places spilling over from small restaurants that also cater to an indoor clientele; semi-enclosed groupings of eateries near 'wet markets' where people frequently shop for the freshest ingredients; and fragrant, loud and spatially fluid restaurants that seem soldered onto one another in the shadow of tall housing estates, where the majority of Hong Kong residents now live after a half-century of public housing programmes. Although these three categories help to make sense of big-sign eateries in Hong Kong, many *daipaidongs* do not fit neatly into one of the three typological boxes. Instead, the largely organic way in which these places were established, and then evolved in the midst of Hong Kong's dynamic shifts, suggests surprises in their form, quality and peculiarities.

We encountered the first type – an unpretentious, belly-filling place tucked away in an alley – late one night in 1987, when we first arrived in Hong Kong jet-lagged after a long transpacific journey. Sleepless in a strange city, we yearned to taste Asia and looked for night food near our small hotel in Kowloon. We

followed some fluorescent lights in the kind of grimy, crowded neighbourhoods one might recognise from gritty Hong Kong action movies. The air was laden with moisture and we immediately worked up a sweat. Older men in T-shirts and shorts talked to each other as they sat on stools under a crude canvas canopy. The fare was vegetables and noodles in a rich broth. We immediately knew we were in Asia, in part because of the not-quite-indoor, not-quite-outdoor nature of the little alley where we satisfied our hunger.

Fortunately, many of these eateries have survived in contemporary Hong Kong. They don't usually advertise their dishes on large signs, but the dishes are often similar to what can be found in larger outdoor *daipaidong*s. Furthermore, the smaller, alley-hugging, dining 'holes in the [urban] wall' often change their personalities according to the time of day. From early morning till lunchtime, they confine themselves to four interior-facing walls. However, by evening (like restaurant larvae climbing out of their shells), they spill into alleys, onto sidewalks or even into the middle of streets where passing clients are tempted by their smells and sights. One can find a dispersed constellation of these kinds of 'urban dining rooms' in some of the older neighbourhoods of Mongkok and Yaumatei – on the

Kowloon side of Hong Kong harbour – as well as in some of the side streets of Wanchai and Sheung Wan on Hong Kong island.

To savour the second kind of *daipaidong*, one has to look near 'wet markets' where, until supermarkets began undercutting the markets' traditional appeal in the past quarter-century, most Hong Kong residents shopped for fresh and dried produce, meat, fish and much more. Similar to urban configurations the world over, cooked-food retailing in Hong Kong dovetailed easily with raw-food marketing. One of the former colony's more unusual *daipaidongs* is attached to the wet market at North Point on Hong Kong island. It occupies the upper floor of the three-storey structure that houses the market. In the evening, when the market stalls are dormant, one can climb the concrete steps up to the *daipaidong* level, hear deafening roars of laughter and dishes clattering, and see wall-to-wall food revellers who savour the fresh food cooked on the spot in large woks. Hong Kong's urban density is found here in delicious microcosm.

Similar kinds of spatial configurations – big-sign eateries cheek by jowl with colourful markets – can be found throughout Hong Kong. Some of the most notable are along Temple Street in Kowloon, where shopping, fortune-telling and Cantonese opera-singing thrive in harmonious juxtaposition with people of all ages who sit outdoors with friends, eating fresh seafood, animal intestines and a rich array of vegetables or other culinary temptations.

The third variation on the big-sign theme – as a series of symbiotically attached restaurants fanning out from a central core of separate kitchens – occurs in association with several public housing estates, most of which were built from the early 1960s to the late 1990s. Hong Kong's public housing programmes were initiated after the Second World War, when the colony's so-called 'free economy' mushroomed, and especially after 1949 when the People's Republic of China was established, thus setting the stage for a flood of refugees who streamed across the border for the next quarter-century.

The British, unprepared for this influx, were caught unawares when many refugees settled in ramshackle shantytowns on urban hillsides. But on Christmas Eve 1953, when a tragic fire ravaged one of those settlements at Shek Kip Mei and hundreds died, the British government was shamed into confronting the challenge of how to house the refugees (and many others). It began to construct housing units in high-rise concrete towers. Designers and planners included provisions for markets, buses and other necessities. And because the initial housing units were only about 300 square feet (without dining rooms), with shared kitchens along public corridors, one of those necessities quickly became the creation of eating spaces where friends and families could congregate more comfortably. The traditional *daipaidong* thus morphed into another configuration – an urban mega-dining-room that lured residents with inexpensive, freshly cooked and delicious food. It is plebeian fare that many still seek.

Our personal favourite of this third type of *daipaidong* is at the Wo Che housing estate, near Sha Tin in the New Territories. Anchored to a concrete plaza in the middle

Above left
From street level, the beckoning, illuminated Wo Che *daipaidong* is perched slightly above the concreted open spaces between the housing blocks.

Above right
Viewed from above, the Wo Che *daipaidong* is sandwiched between high-rise housing blocks. Its corrugated tin roof is extended even further thanks to canvas awnings. Trees rise above the concrete plaza, where tables from one restaurant splay outward beyond interior confines.

The big-sign *daipaidong*, then, is but one manifestation of a Hong Kong identity that has evolved from Chinese culture. Restaurants of many cuisines thrive in Hong Kong, but if one looks beyond the conventional four walls of a standard restaurant, one can see how the city itself sometimes becomes one remarkable dining room.

Above left
This imposing creation – brightly coloured paper festooning a temporary bamboo structure – signals a *daipaidong* restaurant under new ownership. Many new restaurants in Hong Kong launch their ventures in this way, hoping to catch the attention of customers who almost always have their senses bombarded as they make their way through a day of hyper-intense city life.

Above right
Tableside, one can see some of the characteristic features of *daipaidong* dining: big signs heralding the day's dishes, fluorescent lights, round tables covered with thin plastic sheets, toilet-paper rolls encased in plastic holders, and either tea or water in plastic containers. The transparency of the boundary between one restaurant and an adjoining one is also evident here.

of a thicket of 20-storey housing blocks, this *daipaidong* is a sprawling, loose conglomeration of attached restaurants. In the evening, when the place bursts with life, servers beckon passers-by (potential customers) to come and sit down and enjoy dishes such as steaming hotpots, fried calamari and shrimp steamed with copious amounts of garlic, or duck and taro root simmered with coconut milk to perfection in clay pots.

Those who stop – sometimes including motorcyclists who park their shiny hogs nearby – choose from tables under the *daipaidong*'s corrugated tin roof near a blaring TV elevated above the fray, alongside friends who are already there. Fluorescent lights ablaze, the servers pour tea onto table tops so that paper-thin sheets of plastic might stick to them and cover the table, though this occurs with varying degrees of success. The napkins are toilet rolls sheathed in plastic dispensers (in the more upmarket *daipaidongs*). Big signs frame the scene, with Chinese characters in different fonts luring the hungry with tantalising possibilities. Young women servers – often referred to as 'beer girls' – cajole customers to buy their particular brand of cold beer at a reduced price. The heaping dishes arrive and are consumed with gusto.

Any number of customers can be accommodated at Wo Che; round table-tops can be rolled out instantaneously so that a small table for four can quickly and easily seat 16. The borders between private *daipaidong* and public space beyond are blurred. It is a dining room without

walls, a feast without fanfare, a tradition without pretension, affordable for those living in public housing.

Many Hong Kong residents eat the majority of their meals outside their homes, in part because of convenience (Hong Kong boasts about 30,000 eating places in a city of 7 million), time considerations ('fast food' is often prepared hyper-quickly) and a widespread desire by many Hong Kongers to socialise with others whilst eating, rather than remain solitary. The big-sign *daipaidong*, then, is but one manifestation of a Hong Kong identity that has evolved from Chinese culture. Restaurants of many cuisines thrive in Hong Kong, but if one looks beyond the conventional four walls of a standard restaurant, one can see how the city itself sometimes becomes one remarkable dining room. Take a seat and you will not only eat, but also experience Hong Kong's human vitality as a dynamic garnish.

Recently, the Hong Kong government has relaxed some restrictions over alfresco dining, which is a shot in the arm for *daipaidong* survival. At the same time, however, *daipaidongs* are no longer permitted in newly constructed areas. The gentrification of urban areas, stricter hygiene laws and the desire of many to eat in air-conditioned places have also threatened the survival of the *daipaidong*. In the increasingly pervasive mall culture of the former colony, a franchise called 'Daipaidong' has perverted the vernacular place and made it more polished and upmarket. Many of those residents who yearn for the bygone *daipaidong* are increasingly becoming aware of how casually the smaller-scale manifestations of Hong Kong identity, the *daipaidong* among them, are being eradicated in the name of property development and urban renewal. ⚏

Blurring Boundaries, Defining Places:
The New Hybrid Spaces of Eating

Restaurants and food franchises have become ubiquitous in public spaces around the world, whether one is visiting a museum or concert hall in Europe, Asia or North America, or places of interchange, such as railway stations and airports. **Gail Satler** discusses the spatial and social transformation that the placement and design of these dining spaces and food stalls have effected, as they invite and guide movement not only within their immediate environment, but also across the greater cityscape.

Above
Michael Jordan's Steakhouse, Grand Central Terminal, New York, The Rockwell Group, 1998–9
Rich tones, dimmed lighting and sweeping screen-walls heighten the feeling of elegance and status initiated by the restaurant's siting on the balconies.

The presence of restaurants in venues such as museums, concert halls, airports and train stations is not new. What has changed over the past five years or so are the kinds of spatial and social relationships such restaurants have fostered. Instead of closing off from, or blending into, the dominant spaces, restaurants contest traditional relationships and existing boundaries by using design features that shift the temporal, as well as the spatial, parameters.

Whilst designed to enable users to easily move in and out of the larger space, these restaurants are also designed to offer new vistas and intentions, as well as new rhythms. By doing so, they achieve a sense of real time and place in spaces that are otherwise placeless (a blur) or iconic (static). Their identity is as dependent on connectivity and easy transition as it is on shifting patterns of movement and visibility. As such, their connectivity forms an experiential path in and out of the larger built form, creating a truly hybrid space.

This spatial transformation references broader relational shifts occurring in the larger context in which hybrid spaces are often found: cities. As cities expand their reach and connect to other cities through global networks of exchange (in commerce and communication), balancing global and local processes becomes a primary concern. There is a growing need to accommodate the local resident and worker along with what sociologist Guido Martinotti identifies as the new city user.[1] This user, the middle-class business person/tourist, lives between cities rather than in any particular one. Such users are of tremendous importance, not just for global cities, but for smaller cities engaged in the ever-expanding market economy.

How does one translate the idea of a global economy (or society) which exists everywhere yet nowhere into the physical structures of a specific place? And how does one appeal to the local as well as the global user?

Restaurants, especially those found in public settings that serve both user types, can become a locus for exploring these questions. As places of consumption, restaurants have to catch and hold the attention of customers. And as places that offer a way to make use of the time 'in between' other activities and spaces, they take on the dual role of facilitating easy movement whilst also creating enough interest to temporarily alter pedestrian flow and dominant spatial pattern. Working in a manner similar to filters or semipermeable membranes,

In airports and train terminals, which emphasise hypermobility and hyperconnectivity verging on pure virtuality, the transformation entails slowing people down and engaging, rather than merely distracting, them while they wait. One way in which this is accomplished is by getting people to move off the main thoroughfare or grid without losing connection to it.

controlling and regulating movement across the larger terrain of the dominant space and the larger cityscape, restaurants help draw the eye to an image or place offering a new perspective, and with it the possibility of reinterpreting the meaning of the whole.[2]

Going Vertical

In airports and train terminals, which emphasise hypermobility and hyperconnectivity verging on pure virtuality, the transformation entails slowing people down and engaging, rather than merely distracting, them while they wait. One way in which this is accomplished is by getting people to move off the main thoroughfare or grid without losing connection to it.

In New York City's Grand Central Terminal, for example, the traditional use of upper and lower levels is enlisted to denote differences in status, so that restaurants sited on the terminal's balconies offer higher-end dining experiences, whilst the dining concourse, located on the lower level, 'offers a selection of more moderately priced ... informal restaurants and snacking choices for eating in or taking out'.[3] Both venues serve commuters, neighbourhood businesspeople and out-of-town visitors.

The marble stairways branching off the main concourse to the east and west balconies serve as transitional cues for the shift in motion and place for both diners and onlookers. In venues that include Michael Jordan's Steakhouse, Cipriani Dolce, Metrazur and the Campbell Apartment, diners can see and be seen by those passing through the terminal's main concourse. Semifixed features help enhance the restaurants and their patrons, distinguishing them from other spaces and users of the terminal. They also increase the privacy of diners within the restaurant, something which could not be addressed structurally due to the landmark status of the building. This is in contrast to the terminal's Oyster Bar and Restaurant

Top
**Dining concourse, Grand
Central Terminal, New York,
The Rockwell Group, 1998–9**
The Rockwell Group created
custom chairs and tables to
provide the look of a living
room for the dining concourse.
Pullman-car-style seating,
which radiates outwards from
the central core, is available
for those opting for the fast-
food choices, and numerous
retail kiosks are geared
towards the last-minute needs
of travellers.

Right
**Figs, LaGuardia Airport, New
York, Niemitz Group, 2001**
Distinct dining spaces offer a
choice of options to the diner
and create a strong character
for a restaurant without a
defined perimeter.

Above
**Concession Triangle, Midway
Airport, Chicago, A Epstein &
Sons International with design
architects Santec Architecture,
2001–4**
The concession triangle
suggests a Chicago street in
form and content, right down to
the 'sidewalk seating' that is
designed to look much like it
does on the city's sidewalks.

(1913) on the lower level. While certainly considered elegant, the restaurant was until recently almost completely closed off from the rest of the terminal and also quite noisy. Entry to it felt like a descent into the catacombs.

Entry into the new lower-level dining concourse offers a very different experience. It is also achieved by the use of elegant marble stairways, but these are less visually available than those on the main concourse. As users descend, they make several turns, spiralling off-grid. This creates a more dramatic physical and temporal transition from grid to the 'space below', and evokes a sense of expectation regarding what lies around the corner. Functionally, these shifts increase quiet and privacy from the main concourse without totally disconnecting from it.

The dining concourse is designed to be multipurpose: part living room and part dining space. The custom-designed living-room-style seating is arranged to face the stairways and the action pathways that function as city streets, as it circumscribes the central food court.

The feel of the dining concourse is that of a neighbourhood street of New York City. This includes ethnic diversity in the cuisine, vibrant

colours, multisensory stimulation and a sense of bustle. Here, one can be alone in the crowd, yet, as on city streets, with the possibility of fleeting chance encounters. Varying intensities of lighting, and seating to accommodate both singles and groups through the use of communal tables or counters with stools facing towards or away from the street and stairways, reinforce the duality of the urban experience.

The terminal's diverse eating options work well precisely because they are so different. Juxtaposing their physical proximity with their social distance reinforces the designers' intention that the terminal reflect the surrounding city as a place of hierarchy, social mobility and asymmetrical spatial and social relationships.

However, verticality can also challenge such relationships and distinctions. When creatively approached, traditional assumptions can be turned on their heads. In New York City's LaGuardia Airport, for example, part of the restaurant Figs' cachet is generated by its situation below ground whilst visibility from ground level is maintained. Having only one wall and no ceiling creates a high degree of connection with the rest of the terminal. But its location at the bottom of escalators that descend from the departure gates creates a path that is not part of the natural flow of the airport. Thus, physical and

visual connection is countered by moving off the grid and below ground.

In addition to visibility, Figs makes use of design features and materials that counter the sleek modern sense of the airport to lure people in. Large-scale furniture in the form of a log bar, leather seats and maple perimeter knee walls along with fig trees, create a sense of permanence and enclosure without entirely closing off the space. These features act as screens rather than walls, heightening the dining experience and again providing a sense of being seen but not being totally within reach.

Staying on the Street: Locality

Using the street as site as well as vista can create a sense of locality. By offering seating that spills onto the main thoroughfare, the pathway becomes the stage for interaction as much as for movement in much the same way that local streets do in cities. That is, the line between outside and inside, between actor and audience, is obscured and more fluid. The concession triangle in Chicago's newly renovated Midway Airport was designed precisely with this in mind. What localises the concession triangle and distinguishes it from the type of food court traditionally found in shopping malls or airports is that the venues are unique and specific to Chicago. Most of them are offshoots of restaurants located elsewhere in the city. While they resemble the 'original', modifications are made to accommodate the context and the user.

In some cases there is an eat-in and takeaway version of the eatery in the same airport. The creation of one-offs is a growing trend, so finding examples of this in the 'new cities' – in airports or in train stations – should not be surprising. Care was taken to select venues that represent the city's diversity, for example in food style, by neighbourhood and by price-point.

Locality is further enhanced by the use of symbols that evoke individual and collective memories. Symbols of the past offer opportunities for people to remember or be taken back in time through small gestures such as photos or decor within the restaurant, or by the choice of the restaurants themselves. Figs, for example, was designed to recreate the taste and feel of 'the great neighbourhood pizzerias' chef/owner Todd English frequented in the Bronx whilst visiting extended family when he was growing up, 'where they all knew us and where we became sort of part of the family'.[4] Creating the sense of neighbourhood and of family become important in a venue such as an airport, which is devoid of either.

The goal of literally injecting a taste of Chicago into Midway's eating concession is achieved by using some of Chicago's traditional or long-standing venues. Both gestures use history to reinforce a sense of place. Restaurants, in effect, act as a bridge between periphery (airport) and centre (the city). They help fill the gap between, as writer Pico Iyer suggests, 'what community yearns to be as well as what it really is'.[5]

Bringing the Outside In

In places such as concert halls or museums, where the intention of the space is to freeze a moment or elevate place and experience to the status of the monumental, restaurants can restore dynamism and human scale. One way in which this is accomplished is by bringing the outside in; that is, offering visual access to the outside cityscape. And when gardens, visual or other multisensory connections to the cityscape are included, restaurants can transcend the structural envelope to embrace both the landscape outside and the furniture inside. Both gestures help orient the hybrid space to the organic line of the larger urban landscape, reminding us that a landscape is a landscape, whether built or natural.

The Rhapsody restaurant in Chicago's Symphony Center and Michael Jordan's in Grand Central Terminal are examples of such spaces. Both use varying colour palettes, natural and artificial lighting and expansive windows to distinguish and connect their eating spaces to one another and to the outside. Rhapsody consists of three eating spaces: the bar area, the conductor's room and the urban garden. Moving from Rhapsody's bar area, amber and brown with dim golden light, to the conductor's room, yellow and pale green with natural light streaming in from the wall of glass which can be opened onto the urban garden, makes the transition fluid and lively. The urban garden emphasises the natural greens but uses accents of yellow to connect it to the conductor's room. Lighting fixtures in the garden interface with those on Wabash Street, helping to connect the space to the larger cityscape.

The unlikely siting of the garden here offers an element of surprise and delight for restaurant patrons, as well as for those who come upon it from Wabash Street. Sitting low to the ground, the urban garden contests the glass, steel and concrete high-rises and built forms that surround it. By design and context, the garden is a flower that blooms amid their shadows.

Michael Jordan's Steakhouse similarly uses shifts of colour and the luminosity of space to move people from the bar and dining areas on the balcony into the more private dining space. Here, the outside is brought in symbolically but effectively. To give Michael Jordan's the feel of a dining club-car, architect David Rockwell adopted details from the grand design of the Twentieth Century Limited train by Raymond Loewy. One external feature of the 'outside' that both Rhapsody and Michael Jordan's incorporate is trains. Both incorporate trains (and mobility) into their designs as well as their vistas. Their siting may seem an unlikely relationship between the ordinary activity of commuting and elegant dining, but it is precisely this relationship that heightens the connection, albeit an asymmetrical one, between two vital features of cities today.

Conclusion

Blurring need not reduce identity. Acting as asymmetrical conduits of movement and difference, restaurants can take people to places they might not have considered going to before. Using the energy and texture of their surroundings in their design whilst injecting new elements and perspectives with which to understand dominant and peripheral spaces, restaurants become sites where local and global, social and physical parameters intersect and interact. As such, they remind us that connectivity may be understood in the social as well as in the physical sense. By altering the traditional rhythm and flow, restaurants can allow us to view a space more thoroughly than we would if we were drawn directly to the vanishing point of traditional perspective. In this way, restaurants can counter global forces that often deny the importance of local cultures in the marketplace and in cities themselves. ⌂

Below left
Michael Jordan's Steakhouse, Grand Central Terminal, New York, The Rockwell Group, 1998–9
The curves of the screens and banquettes, the richness of the beautifully lit metal-leaf cornice and the velvets and leathers of the furniture frame, and are framed by, the grand windows and the domed sky-ceiling of the terminal.

Below right
Urban garden, Rhapsody, Symphony Center, Chicago, Aria Architects, 1997
The facade for the garden area, inspired by metro stations in Paris, helps give it an urban edge and connects the space with the elevated train above it.

Notes
1 Guido Martinotti, 'The New Morphology of Cities', online edition, February 1994. See www.unesco.org/most/wien/guido.htm.
2 Alex S MacLean, *Designs on the Land: Exploring America From the Air*, Thomas & Hudson (New York), 2003, p 131.
3 Rockwell Group materials. See www.rockwellgroup.com.
4 2001 winner: Figs Restaurant, online edition. See www.HotConcepts! Awards.txt.
5 Pico Iyer, *The Global Soul*, Vintage (New York), 2000, p 6.

Out of the Kitchen and onto the Footpath

In Brisbane, southeast Queensland, the number of people eating out in restaurants has increased almost fourfold in just over a decade. The emergence of public dining places on the footpaths has reinvented the city. **Louisa Carter** looks beyond the attractive veneer of well-clipped vegetation and heritage street furniture to the socioeconomic and political forces behind the development, and asks whether as a trend it is effectively cocooning urban residents 'in comfort and convenience' and is in danger of creating an artificial urban panacea.

Until recently, Brisbane was probably considered a second-tier capital city in Australia where, historically, development opportunism has been followed by infrastructure. Whilst to its residents this region is still all about thunderstorms in the late afternoon, and bats in the mango trees at night, a quiet but obvious transformation of the space of the public street has been under way. Now, the urban practices of the café set have spread throughout the suburbs, attaching to existing retail space in a relatively seamless transition.

In 1990, the Brisbane telephone directory listed 532 restaurants; today they number over 2,000. Staking out highly visible locations on the city's footpaths, in a far-flung emulation of a European ideal, outdoor dining has blossomed from pavement after pavement. Like a series of signboards, groupings of tables and chairs beckon residents to sample the new leisure life.

'Isn't it wonderful?' we remark. 'Isn't it making the city more "livable"?' we observe. 'How did it happen?' Nobody asks. 'What are the implications?' Nobody cares.

Taking a step back from the enormous popularity of the outdoor dining spaces in Brisbane, we need to consider their materiality and cultural impact. We need to remember who we are, consider where these places are taking us and what forces have influenced their delivery. Outdoor dining forms a visible and accessible element of consumption communities.[1] Whilst at one level it is a continuation of the rituals of display, sensualism and sociability that have always surrounded dining practices, at another level it is the process by which this practice has been fostered that deserves attention.

Facilitated by changes in regulations regarding the footpaths of both urban and suburban areas, this cultural and spatial revolution has been very much planned for, and encouraged, by the local government authorities in and around Brisbane. As with bread and circuses, local governments have hit upon a successful strategy to foster a new leisure life.

From Restaurant to Footpath

Historically, in southeast Queensland public outdoor food consumption has been limited to picnics in a landscape setting, quick fuelling-up at snack bars and fish-and-chips shops, or a steak sandwich accompanying copious amounts of alcohol in a hotel beer garden. Prior to the 1980s/1990s, dining experiences were generally limited to either fine dining rooms or tearooms. Both of these spaces were traditionally closeted away from the dust and glare of the street, often with deep plush furnishings or fine linen cloths. In the prewar era, menus were generally simple English fare, and these were places where one used a napkin and said please. Tea was served in bone china, and sandwiches were small and crafted.

After the Second World War, and accompanied by the introduction of the motor car as an affordable form of independence and mobility, outdoor eating experiences were concentrated in the holiday areas or tourist locations. In contrast, the city tearooms, such as the Rose Arcade Tea Room, the Shingle Inn and the Cubana, were all separated from the outside world, with few or no windows to the street – places where quiet conversation and a retreat from the hustle and bustle of the town could be found.

In the late 1960s and 1970s, the most fashionable restaurants in Brisbane – Michael's (formerly the Camellia) and the Milano – were intensely internalised, cool, air-conditioned spaces with lush modern furnishings in natural tones, soft lighting and mirrors, and completely removed from the outside world. Dining was something special, private and intentional, an experience where one was required to be well dressed and to speak in hushed tones.

Perhaps a precursor to public outdoor dining was the hotel beer garden, a place where the whole family could go for a meal at the local hotel. The beer garden was also made possible through changes to liquor licensing legislation in the 1950s, which allowed alcohol to be served outdoors. These spaces took advantage of the region's temperate weather. Partially covered, situated at the rear of the hotel, and generally far from the street, they were casual and open, but nevertheless reserved for hotel patrons only.

With the arrival of World Expo '88, Brisbane came of age as a city, changing from a big old country town to a

The New Cafe

Readers will be pleased to know that a dainty Cafe has just been opened by Griffiths Bros.; in Queen Street, just below the Post Office. This photograph shows the interior of the artistic tea rooms.

Opposite
A young father minds the sleeping baby as a phone call is made.
Their companion leafs through the Sunday paper.

Right
Griffith Brothers tearoom, Queen Street, Brisbane, 1929
Tearooms of the early 20th century were removed from the dust and glare of the street.

modern metropolis that held international appeal. Expo showed Brisbane residents of the late 20th century that they could get out of their quiet suburban homes and enjoy a communal outdoor life. Identifiable by its huge 'sails' along the river front, the Brisbane World Expo created a taste for an urban lifestyle, where Brisbane people learnt about a form of casual and accessible leisure based neither on the formal arts nor sport.

Outdoor dining in Brisbane intensified after the expo. The Central Business District maintained its extended opening hours. Once limited to between 9am and 5pm weekdays, and

9am and noon on Saturdays, shops could open from 9am until 9pm on Friday nights, from 9am until 4pm on Saturdays and from 10am until 4pm on Sundays. Emerging alongside these extended shopping hours in the city was the need for increasing numbers of food establishments, particularly in the form of fast-food outlets, tearooms and cafés. Along with the redevelopment of the expo site (which became the Southbank Parklands in 1992), the central-city region of Brisbane was established as an after-hours venue for drinking and dining out. Both the Southbank Parklands and the Queen Street Mall acted as precursors to the plethora of local leisure places now located throughout most of the city, places which have an emphasis on

Top left
A small element with a big impact – the sale of public space for private profit is set out between brass plaques throughout the outdoor dining localities in Brisbane.

Top right
Bulimba Bean, Oxford Street, Bulimba, Brisbane
The Bulimba Bean stretches beyond the boundaries of its ownership. Extra space means extra dollars in a burgeoning suburban economy.

Right
The Colony Club, Brisbane, 1966
The Colony Club was consistent with dining spaces of its time in Brisbane, which favoured modern furnishings, mirrors, wall-to-wall carpets and removal from the street .

outdoor relaxation, landscape amenity, shade structures and the café lifestyle.

Since that time, Brisbane's streets have blossomed with small café and restaurant tenancies, providing a lifestyle of intracity tourism where suburbanites go out to the neighbourhoods of Logan Road, Stones Corner, Racecourse Road, Ascot or Oxford Street in Bulimba to sit around, chat and dine on the city's footpaths. This new use of public space has transformed the city's traditional street-based shopping areas, which were suffering the economic impact of the popularity of the larger American-style suburban shopping centres.

The most popular footpath dining areas are generally those that have been subject to a range of streetscape improvements, either through direct capital-works expenditure by the local government authorities, or through private development undertaking street beautification beyond the boundaries of its own site. These traditional high streets now appear more active; but, as accessible novelties in the suburban landscapes in which they are located, they are served by a market reaching well beyond their own local suburban catchment. Often characterised by their consistent streetscape treatments, furniture, menus and style of decor, and tenanted by chain-store cafés, many of the outdoor dining offers in the region remain substantially similar to those of the others.[2]

Moving well beyond a space for food consumption, outdoor dining has transformed urban life in Brisbane and the region. Local government regulations have been reviewed to enable the consumption of alcohol and food in public, and to make those public spaces available for rent by private entrepreneurs for their own benefit. Dining on the public footpath is not something seen historically in this part of the world, and its proliferation in the last 15 years is culturally remarkable.

Out of the Kitchen
Substantial social, demographic and economic changes in the latter part of the 20th century have all contributed to the acceptance of outdoor dining activities in Brisbane and southeast Queensland in general. In particular, both men and women are marrying later and divorcing in greater numbers, more people are studying as the work place becomes highly competitive and less stable, retirees are not content to garden and listen to the radio all day long, there has been a growth in the number of part-time workers, divorcees are dating for the second

or third time around, young mothers are out and about, stressed workers are looking for temporary relief, and many of the under-30s want to enjoy themselves rather than save a deposit for a house.

All of these groups are using the city in a different way, one that responds to their needs for flexibility in time and space. Their 'family room' is found on every café chair, and whilst they want to feel like they belong, they still want to retain their anonymity, cycling from one outdoor dining locale to the next as if they were tourists in their own town. Ensconced in their new family room, they do not need large houses for entertaining, nor to be fabulous cooks. They are out of their kitchens and onto the footpaths, reading newspapers, having breakfast, having dinner, talking to friends on the phone, spending time with their 'neighbours' and just generally relaxing.

Local public outdoor-dining space has reinvented the city, creating moments of public activity in a predominantly privatised suburban landscape. With average footpath widths at approximately 3.5 to 4 metres, and after a history of local government restrictions on street stalls and other hawking activities, up to half the width, or more, of the public right of way outside a food establishment is now available for rent by the private sector. Initially supported through amendments in the Queensland state government's Traffic Act in 1990, local governments in southeast Queensland went on to amend their own footpath dining and goods-on-roadway regulations throughout the 1990s. Intended to regulate the health, safety and insurance aspects of the new practice, these early regulatory adjustments are now supported by detailed design requirements.

The result is a footpath zone, generally kerbside, where a restaurant or café tenancy is able to place tables, chairs, planters, screens for protection from the weather, and signage. Whilst rents are paid to local governments, the cost of the space in comparison with on-site table space is nominal. The ordinary footpath user must now carefully negotiate all sorts of obstructions in the reduced pavement area: menu boards, chair legs, cigarettes held away from other diners, waiters conveying food and drink across their paths of travel, babies' prams and the intrusive gaze of the urban voyeur, have all dramatically changed this space in the city.

The surfaces and finishes of the outdoor dining areas in southeast Queensland generally present as larger-scale interpretations of the suburban patio – paved or exposed aggregate ground surfaces, potted plants, awning covers, tree planting and outdoor furniture settings. The spaces are generally said to be 'human scale' and 'local'. They are repetitive with variations on the same theme, incorporating subtle changes in detail, colour and planting. They are not unique when

Right
Bulimba Bean, Oxford Street, Bulimba, Brisbane
Patio roofs, electric fans, potted plants, roll-down plastic blinds ... The result remains very suburban in Oxford Street, Bulimba.

Notes
1 Professor Brendon Gleeson, 'The Future of Australia's Cities: Making Space for Hope', professorial lecture delivered on Griffith University's Nathan Campus, Brisbane, June 2004.
2 There are, of course, exceptions, such as the James Street Market Precinct, but the most numerous and visible outdoor dining areas are those attached to traditional retail shopping streets.
3 James Coutts, 'Brisbane Revives its Suburban Centres', *Landscape Australia* 2, 1999, pp 95–8.
4 Clive Hamilton, 'Why the Well-Off Feel Hard Done By: the Politics of Affluence', *Sydney Morning Herald*, 30 November 2002.
5 Richard Rees, 'Planning on the Edge', *Urban Design Forum*, No 65, March 2004.
6 Gleeson, op cit.
7 Sharon Zukin, *Landscapes of Power: From Detroit to Disney World*, University of California Press (Berkeley, CA), 1991, p 268.
8 Diane Caney 'inside/outside intertextuality' (www.overthere.com.au/digital/textfields.html) in discussion of the work of Julia Kristeva, *Desire in Language: A Semiotic Approach to Literature and Art*, Basil Blackwell (Oxford), 1984.
9 See *Henri Lefebvre Writings on Cities*, trans Eleonore Kofman and Elizabeth Lebas (eds), Basil Blackwell (Oxford), 1996, pp 111–46 for an interesting discussion on these matters.

considered comparatively and, as a type of space in this region, the landscape and design outcomes retain strong references to their surrounding suburbia. Even though the café uses are in place, from a material perspective these suburban renovations of the city's footpaths have done little to urbanise their localities, maintaining a strong provincial character where 'other' is not part of the approved aesthetics or practices.

Outdoor dining spaces are generally attached to other consumption opportunities for retail and leisure (for example, cinemas). They are rarely attached to parks, places of scenic beauty or views. In reality, the places where outdoor dining is most extensive is along roads, where the noise and airborne pollutants render the spaces uninhabitable when one examines Australian Standards and the food and hygiene regulations. So what drives these suburban living rooms where some comfort must be found, despite their obvious flaws?

Middle-Class Welfare?

Continuing a long tradition of government gift-giving over the centuries, local governments in southeast Queensland have set about beautifying traditional retail centres, ostensibly in a bid to stimulate their economic vitality and to improve neighbourhood amenity.[3] At face value, these initiatives are positive insertions into the suburban fabric which foster a new community connectedness, but underneath their notable homogeneity is a range of strategies aimed at both supporting and rewarding the good citizen. Middle-class welfare has typically been what

drives special-interest groups, and at one level street-beautification schemes can be considered in this way in relation to the business owners, the possibility that this form of governance responds to 'luxury fever'[4] deserves consideration.

This is not what is sometimes referred to as an 'ecstatic urbanism',[5] but more of a comfort-feeding chain-store sub-urbanity: a space in the city where the environment is nice, where everything is integrated in an attempt to make an otherwise competitive society relaxed and comfortable for a moment in a manufactured aesthetic exclusion of otherness. Whilst intended to be part of the process and physicality of these places, identity and difference are incorporated only once the suburban aesthetic ideal covers every surface (exposed aggregate and paving), tames the vegetation (neatly planted trees, ground covers and clipped hedges) and filters one's knowledge of the history of the area (through street-furniture design and 'artworks'). These repetitive insertions into the city's fabric provide an assertion of certain values over others. They are an assurance of a particular kind of lifestyle over other kinds. Like a filtering finding, it is here that the middle-classes submissively look for leisure, perhaps rendered insensible to the sameness by the world of change elsewhere.

Even so, with its high levels of sensual amenity (shade, soft landscaping, birds in the trees, the aromas of gourmet food and coffee, soft candlelit table settings and so on), outdoor dining might just be that accessible 'oil change'[6] needed to relieve the stress and competitiveness of modern society, and to create the capacity for a leisured life for the many.

In assessing the positives, we must consider that none of this would have been possible without significant local government support in the form of legislative reform, capital-works investment and marketing. The notable characteristic of these changes has been the reflection of a local, accessible and everyday form of governance. The outcomes are not expensive to create, but are considered highly lucrative (in both monetary and social terms) in their primary and secondary effects. Local government authorities and the development industry have combined their efforts to produce a spatial economy where the new leisure lifestyle is given the credit for transforming other geographical attributes such as land value, demographic tenure and investment potential, to an extent well beyond the previous profile of the places in which they have occurred.

The importance of all this is the issue of force and the scale of it – of governments converging with developers and landowners (who must essentially be driven by the profit motive) to reinvent our local places, inform our aspirations in a contrived suburban theatre-set, and use the public realm of the street as

This is not what is sometimes referred to as an 'ecstatic urbanism', but more of a comfort-feeding chain-store sub-urbanity: a space in the city where the environment is nice, where everything is integrated in an attempt to make an otherwise competitive society relaxed and comfortable for a moment in a manufactured aesthetic exclusion of otherness.

Above
Interpretive streetscape element, artwork or cultural selection? These government-funded and facilitated insertions refer to the textile industry in Stones Corner.

a structuring medium[7] for who we are and what we want. The array of bureaucratic power, in terms of its financial and organisational depth, is in enormous contrast to the decision of an individual not to engage in these power/space relations. An individual's personal choices remain iteratively informed (or limited) by the options that are available, and whilst perhaps they will not be consumed by the force, they are advised by it: 'Here look, this suburban ideal is what is on offer within a dearth of alternatives', and 'What's more, look at all these other people here, this is highly desirable, isn't it?'

These places are not the large monuments traditionally associated with the assertion of power, but everyday spaces repackaged to provide an organisation of the populus at the local level. They are exemplary of a governance of image-making for political effect. Since the product of the engagement is a piece of built environment, 'place' becomes a 'line of force',[8] seemingly irresistible and suckled upon by users unwilling or unable to discern the Disneyfication of space set out before them.

Even though Australians, like people in many other developed societies, are experiencing unprecedented standards of living and personal wealth, our satisfaction with 'near enough' has encouraged the outdoor dining outcomes we have seen. Served up on a McPlatter of relatively repetitive urban and suburban space by local governments and developers in southeast Queensland, outdoor dining is a significant public activity, but it has discernible limits in its current format. The interplay of site-specific culture, food and space found elsewhere in the world is limited here by the design aspects of the relevant regulatory frameworks. Without the freedom to individualise and await the slow development of a place over time, we treat public space as a marketable yet disposable commodity.

A governance of the everyday that targets leisure, choice and our spare time in this way is a powerful pressure, perhaps a cultural violence. Refashioning the city through fetishisation of space[9] as a commodity, this cleansing of socioeconomic difference to promote images of middle-class social conformity stands in the way of our as-yet-unknown aspirations. Instead of an invitation to go no further than the end of one's street, cocooning ourselves in comfort and convenience, surely there is enough space for an edgy, prickly city that sets our hearts racing and our minds alight?

With more than coffee and cake on the menu, outdoor dining in southeast Queensland serves up an extra dose of governance in every bite. Looking beyond the obvious attractiveness of the new practice, we must nevertheless critically evaluate its impacts. Cultivated by administrative agencies and processes, if the city is to be presented for our cultural digestion in this way we must ask to peruse the menu. △

What's Eating Manchester?

Gastro-Culture and Urban Regeneration

Above
Printworks entertainment complex, off Millennium Square, RTKL Architects, 2000
The interior streetscape of the Printworks entertainment complex, home to a multiplex cinema, gym and retail outlets, plus numerous cafés, bars and restaurants. The interior was designed to suggest a neighbourhood of winding streets and shopfronts, and the 'street' links Exchange Square to the city's new transit interchange.

The wide array of new gastronomic establishments in Manchester's city centre symbolise its recent urban regeneration, set in motion by the 1996 IRA bomb that obliterated the Arndale Centre. **David Bell** and Jon Binnie describe the powerful political forces that lie behind this development, and the variety of eating spaces that it has generated, from the Printworks, an entertainment mall in the commercial retail heart, to the Boho shabby chic of the venues in the Northern Quarter.

The regeneration of Manchester's city centre is a widely cited success story; as a result of its enthusiastic embrace of entrepreneurial governance and its vigorous place-promotion campaigns, the centre has been radically transformed over the past two decades, with lavish new consumption spaces, gentrified loft living, revitalised public realms and postindustrial lifestyles centre-staged in its urban renaissance. A powerful emblem of this new Manchester is the development of new spaces of gastronomy and hospitality: restaurants, delicatessens, food halls, bars and clubs. These food spaces are increasingly central to urban regeneration and place-promotion schemes, woven into the experience economy, and used as markers of metropolitanism and cosmopolitanism.

Food and Regeneration
As cities compete with each other to attract capital, businesses and visitors, they are increasingly reoriented to meet the consumption and lifestyle needs of particular groups of people – especially those often referred to as the 'new middle-class' or 'new petite bourgeoisie', a group famed for its reflexive taste-making practices and aestheticisation of everyday life. In the transformation to a postindustrial urban economy, consumption replaces production as the core activity in cities; the key to successful regeneration lies in providing the requisite consumer experiences that act as attractors to the new middle class, and that

transform the patterning of urban life. One central element of this new consumer experience is the production and consumption of urban food spaces: transformations in urban culinary culture can play a paramount role in producing the habitat for ongoing regeneration, and also provide a powerful symbolic statement about urban fortunes. Food and eating are densely and complexly symbolic; the retinue of food spaces on city streets therefore becomes an index of the broader cultures of cities.

In her important book *Landscapes of Power*, American sociologist Sharon Zukin draws a parallel between the transformations to downtown New York since the 1970s, brought about by processes of gentrification, and the rise of nouvelle cuisine: 'gourmet food ... suggests an organization of consumption structurally similar to the deep palate of gentrification.'[1] For Zukin, this equates to the loss of vernacular tradition, and the substitution of a set of standardised 'packages', whether in the form of retrofitted loft apartments or artfully arranged plates of posh nosh. And one of the most problematic effects of this is the chasing-out of other spaces of food, such as older-established cafés. Zukin therefore charts how gentrification and nouvelle cuisine have been twin forces of purification in New York since the 1970s, reshaping the city and what it eats. Certainly, there are signature spaces and signature dishes that have come to signify successful gentrification or regeneration: food spaces associated with 'new' urban lifestyles trade on culinary cultural capital, offering eating experiences that confirm new-middle-class taste formations.

However, Zukin presents a fairly simple process of purification and exclusion. Other studies of gentrifying neighbourhoods and their associated food spaces have shown a more complex and contingent set of processes at work: Alan Latham, for example, has tracked the changing 'hospitality spaces' of one neighbourhood in Auckland, New Zealand, since the early 1990s. He detects a new public culture emerging in cafés, bars and eateries, and writes: 'These food spaces have acted as a key conduit for a new style of inhabiting the city.'[2]

This 'new style' encompasses a cosmopolitan openness and willingness to experiment, a mixing of old and new patterns of sociability and solidarity, and an ethos of 'tolerance, diversity, and creative energy'. While the area has undergone typical processes of gentrification, signified very clearly in the opening of new hospitality spaces such as café-bars, this has

not resulted in the decline or demise of older-established food spaces. The chasing-out that Zukin argues has occurred in downtown New York is not paralleled in Latham's study; instead, a complex and convivial ecology of hospitality spaces has evolved, sustained by, and reflective of, this new style of inhabiting the city.

Manchester's Regeneration Script

Manchester is widely regarded as epitomising a shift towards entrepreneurial governance; a shift in the way in which the city is restructured and promoted, and in the way those processes are managed and financed by both public and private organisations, increasingly working in partnership. As Jamie Peck and Kevin Ward write: 'Manchester has learned how to be very good – some would say the best – at the political theatre of regeneration, with its set-pieces and carefully staged cast.'[3]

The city's regeneration throughout the 1990s was driven by public–private partnerships based on the forging of very close networks of trust between the city council and the local business establishment. These networks had been developed in the city's two unsuccessful bids to host the 1992 and 1996 Olympic Games, and the new form of urban governance shaped by the Olympic bids foreshadowed the business-friendly, New Labour approach to urban regeneration. Other distinctive features of Manchester's regeneration script have included the vigorous promotion of city-centre living, which has attracted over 10,000 people to live in the centre since the mid-1990s. There has also been recognition of the cultural industries as well as institutional support for the development of the city's gay village, recognised as one of the most vibrant and dynamic gay spaces in Europe.

The most vivid testament to Manchester's success in regeneration is the city's response to the IRA bomb that devastated the heart of the commercial area in 1996. Remarkably, the bomb seriously injured only 10 people. However, it badly damaged the heart of retailing in the city centre, including the Arndale Centre – the main shopping centre. It has been estimated that 49,000 square metres of retail space was rendered inoperable by the bomb, and that nearly 700 businesses were forced to relocate. Local politicians and business leaders were quick to realise the opportunity that the disaster provided in terms of redesigning the fabric of the commercial centre of the city. A public–private regeneration company, Manchester Millennium Limited (MML), was established to coordinate the redevelopment, securing funding from the European Regional Development Fund, the city council, central government and the private sector.

The success of MML in attracting public and private investment was reflected in the scale and pace of

Top
Selfridges' flagship city-centre store, Exchange Square, Millennium Quarter, Building Design Partnership and Stanton Williams, 2000
The Millennium Quarter is one of the most recent city-centre regeneration projects in Manchester, providing a mix of upmarket retail and entertainment venues and public-realm enhancements. It includes areas affected by the IRA bombing of the Arndale Centre in June 1996. The overall regeneration project was managed by the Manchester Millennium Limited (MML) partnership, which established the MML Task Force that oversaw the design competition and associated public consultation to redevelop the area.

Right
Selfridges Food Hall, Selfridges, Exchange Square, Future Systems, 2000
Seductive interior view, descending the escalator into the food hall, showing the revolving conveyor-belt servery of the Yo! Sushi counter. Selfridges Food Hall has become an important site in Manchester's new foodscape, offering a range of carefully selected upmarket produce to eat in or take away. The food hall occupies the lower floor of the flagship department store.

rebuilding: within three years, major new public spaces were completed, including the pedestrianised Millennium Square and retail spaces such as the flagship Marks and Spencer store. Towards the end of 2000, the Printworks entertainment complex was opened just off Millennium Square.

While there has been considerable criticism of the outcomes of Manchester's revitalisation, some commentators have also highlighted the city's success stories. Brian Robson, for example, outlines the shape and content of the Manchester 'script' or 'model' of regeneration, including its policy vision for repopulating the city centre through encouraging the development of restaurants, clubs, cinemas, hotels and other leisure and consumption spaces.[4] This strategy has, in Robson's view, successfully transformed urban living in Manchester, creating and sustaining a market for central-city living which has in turn helped to generate a local demand for consumer goods and services, including those related to eating and drinking.

This is certainly true; Manchester is now host to countless shops, bars and restaurants catering to both residents and visitors. This transformation is quite recent, as illustrated by research conducted in the mid-1990s by Ian Taylor and colleagues on the cities of Manchester and Sheffield.[5] In a discussion about shopping in Manchester, focus-group participants told the researchers how difficult it was to find somewhere to get a 'proper' cup of coffee – a statement that seems incredible a decade later, in a city seemingly awash with coffee.

Contrasting Manchester Food Spaces
The Printworks and the Millennium Quarter

The Printworks is an iconic development of one of Manchester's newest additions to its bulging list of 'quarters' – the Millennium Quarter. Opened in 2000 on the site where the printing presses of a national daily newspaper once churned out tabloid headlines, the Printworks is a themed space into which are squeezed a multitude of other themed spaces. The production of themed environments has developed progressively since the 1960s in the West, and involves the use of symbols and motifs that work to convey particular meanings about spaces and places to the people who occupy or use them, and to thereby organise or regulate human activity in accordance with the signification carried by the theming. Most commonly, this means enticing people into acts of consumption through the use of themed motifs connoting pleasure, fun and excitement.[6]

While the Printworks' attractions also include retail outlets, a gym and a state-of-the-art multiplex, it is primarily host to a plethora of themed chain bars and restaurants. The overall feel and look of the Printworks echoes contemporary Las Vegas styling, though the owner and developer describe it as aiming to represent the magic of a film set or stage show. The interior of this entertainment mall is cut through by an indoor

walkway themed as a streetscape, complete with
blue sky and clouds projected onto its 'living
ceiling', heavy use of neon signage, and even a
sidewalk grate which periodically belches steam
in homage to Hollywood's version of New York's
streets. Individual outlets provide a bewildering
array of themed eating and drinking
experiences, again in a Vegas-like vista where
one moves from Ireland to New Orleans in a
matter of footsteps. It also hosts a Hard Rock
Café, a hybrid Indian-Thai-Chinese restaurant,
and a branch of the Wagamama noodle bar,
among its dozen-plus restaurants and 30-plus
bars. The complex is owned by Birmingham-
based private firm Richardson Developments,
who worked with international architects RTKL
to produce a 'story line' encapsulated in the
theming.

The Printworks is, in short, an important hub
in the Millennium Quarter and in the broader
regeneration of Manchester city centre; it draws
in substantial numbers of customers, and is
especially popular with young people. However,
this fact, and the style of its theming, make it
seem strangely at odds with some of the other
spaces of the Millennium Quarter, even if these
are no less themed – spaces such as Urbis, the
city's museum-about-the-city, and the abutting
Exchange Square, home to upmarket retail
outlets. Moreover, the overall theming of the
Printworks as a particular type of consuming-
experience space – dominated by large chain
bars – has brought with it heightened

surveillance and security, with bouncers policing
behaviour, and exacting door policies. In this respect,
then, the Printworks represents a success – in
producing an enticing hospitality space in a previously
neglected part of the city centre that encapsulates the
lively, youth-oriented pleasures of the 24-hour city.
And yet it also shows that producing spaces themed to
attract crowds to eat and drink brings its own problems
for city-centre management.

Loves Saves The Day and the Northern Quarter
Love Saves The Day (LSTD to its regulars) is a deli-cum-
eatery that has come to assume iconic status in the
Northern Quarter and has become a destination deli
for Manchester's gastronomes (there is a second, more
recent branch elsewhere in the city). Since 1999, LSTD
has been housed in one of the ground-floor retail units
in the redeveloped Smithfield Buildings, a loft complex
by local developers Urban Splash, which was completed
in 1998. Its setting, the Northern Quarter, is recognised
as a particularly bohemian Manchester neighbourhood,
famed for its 'shabby chic' mix of small creative
businesses, loft redevelopments, independent retailers
and varied food spaces.[7]

Styled in the postindustrial chic characteristic of the
Smithfield development, LSTD offers a mixture of ready-
prepared food to take home, an eat-in menu and a
small range of deli staples (coffees, teas, condiments).
It also has an extensive wine stock, and regularly holds
wine-tasting evenings as well as themed food nights.
Over the six years since it opened, LSTD has gradually
decreased the floor space given over to shelves of
provisions to take home, and increased space dedicated

to eating on-site: it now has over 50 covers inside, and has more recently expanded outside, offering a few tables on the street, in a 'piazza' tucked between a multistorey car park and adjacent streets. This outdoor eating space represents a curious contact zone, since its tables are often occupied not by LSTD customers, but by homeless people supping cans of cheap lager or just sitting in the sun. In many ways, this is typical of the Northern Quarter, a space that accommodates a diversity of activities and lifestyles that contest claims that it is a wholly gentrified Boho neighbourhood.

Other food spaces in the Northern Quarter echo this mixing: alongside icons of regeneration like LSTD outlets selling low-cost takeaway and eat-in foods, including large numbers of cheap ethnic eateries that have traditionally served the city's immigrant communities, continue to flourish – indeed new ones continue to open up – and 'trendy' bars sit alongside spit-and-sawdust pubs. Just around the corner from LSTD, for example, a small outdoor fruit-and-veg market

Top left
Love Saves The Day, Smithfield Buildings, Northern Quarter, Stephenson Bell Architects, 1999
Interior showing characteristic 'postindustrial chic' design and layout, plus the LSTD branded signage.

Top right
Love Saves The Day's on-street 'piazza', opposite its shopfront on Tib Street. The tables are tucked between a multistorey car park and a substation. The decorated cow on top of the substation is part of Manchester's 2004 Cow Parade, a recent addition to the city's place-promotion calendar.

Right
Ethnic eatery in the Northern Quarter. Rather than being chased out by forces of gentrification, restaurants, cafés and takeaways such as this are thriving, with new venues opening regularly.

offers cheap fresh produce. So, where Zukin saw gentrification chasing out vernacular traditions and lifestyles in downtown New York, what we can see in the Northern Quarter is the rubbing-along of Boho food spaces like LSTD with pre-existing cafés, bars and eateries.

While local concerns are being raised about hikes in rents and business rates leading to smaller businesses being priced out, and some commentators predict a wholesale shift to upmarket consumption spaces in the near future, at present the Northern Quarter perfectly reflects Latham's comment that old and new hospitality spaces can productively coexist in a neighbourhood, helping to produce new patterns of consumption and new ways of urban living – a mixed-use, convivial ecology accommodating the old and the new, tradition and innovation. As Latham found in his study, the most successful of the new food venues opening up managed to connect with pre-existing social and spatial relations, rather than erasing them – and the same can be said for the Northern Quarter.

Conclusion

What these contrasting food spaces reveal, then, is that the transformations brought about by Manchester's regeneration have not resulted solely in a homogenised, purified set of spaces and experiences. Whilst the scale and volume of food spaces has increased remarkably, so has the diversity of consumption sites. The Printworks epitomises the theming approach, in which a sequence of staged experiences is produced in an effort to encourage particular forms of consumption (while also discouraging others). However, even here, we can witness greater differentiation in terms of use than such strict theming is supposed to allow. Love Saves The Day, meanwhile, has nestled into the pre-existing food spaces of the Northern Quarter, and while it has been followed by subsequent waves of Boho bars, cafés and eateries, this influx has not crowded out or priced out older vernacular food spaces in the quarter.

Critics of Manchester's entrepreneurial governance and urban-regeneration agenda tend to overemphasise the purifying tendencies that are argued to erase local distinctiveness and reproduce 'blandscapes' that can be found in cities throughout the world. Whilst there is some truth to this in terms of the serial reproduction of dominant motifs of regeneration schemes in different cities, the textures of use and meaning, the interplay of pre-existing landscapes and lifestyles with those promoted by regeneration and gentrification, suggest that food and regeneration can combine in complex ways to produce – at least sometimes, in some places – those new patterns of urban living that Latham describes. Whether or not the Northern Quarter's convivial ecology is sustainable in the longer term, given current anxieties over rent increases, remains to be seen. But from the evidence of newly opening low-cost eateries in the quarter, it seems that the area is currently able to sustain a mixture of food spaces. Far from being simply eaten up by regeneration, these food spaces continue to offer a varied and tasty platter, not to mention equally diverse eating experiences, thereby feeding the processes of Manchester's urban transformation. ∆

Below
The Barrows market, Northern Quarter
This small street-market is just around the corner from Love Saves The Day. Pre-existing food spaces coexist with newer businesses in this mixed-use neighbourhood.

Notes
1 Sharon Zukin, *Landscapes of Power: From Detroit to Disney World*, University of California Press (Berkeley), 1991, p 206.
2 Alan Latham, 'Urbanity, lifestyle and making sense of the new urban cultural economy: notes from Auckland, New Zealand', *Urban Studies* 40 (9), 2003, pp 1710 and 1706.
3 Jamie Peck and Kevin Ward, 'Placing Manchester', in Jamie Peck and Kevin Ward (eds), *City of Revolution: Restructuring Manchester*, Manchester University Press (Manchester), 2002, p 6.
4 Brian Robson, 'Mancunian ways: the politics of regeneration', in Jamie Peck and Kevin Ward, op cit, pp 34–49.
5 Ian Taylor, Karen Evans and Penny Fraser, *A Tale of Two Cities: Global Change, Local Feeling and Everyday Life in the North of England*, Routledge (London), 1996.
6 For a thorough discussion of the production and consumption of themed environments, see Mark Gottdeiner, *The Theming of America: Dreams, Visions, and Commercial Spaces*, Westview (Boulder, CO), 1997.
7 For a recent review of the Northern Quarter, see Anthony Quinlan, 'Bohemian like you', *City Magazine* 27, pp 29–32.

Acknowledgements
Thanks to Karen Franck for helpful comments and feedback during the writing of this article, and to Abid Qayum for assistance with processing the photographs.

Designing the Gastronomic Quarter

Throughout the world, urban gastronomic quarters, centred on fresh-food markets, have been pulled back from the brink of extinction. Susan Parham explains how movements like Slow Food and Slow Cities in Italy, and the international demand for organic produce, have started to challenge the global food network of production and consumption. The growing revitalisation of urban quarters around produce markets not only serves customers seeking fresh produce, food products and lively cafés and restaurants, but also offers valuable lessons in urban design.

The narrow street runs between high building walls and shuttered windows. Here and there, small shopfronts boast intricate window displays of groceries and fresh produce: a hairy, wild-boar leg wrapped in delicate gold-and-white paper, monogrammed packets of pasta and risotto rice, boxes of chickpeas and lentils, tins of tomatoes and tuna *ventresca*, a profusion of salamis and hams hanging from the ceiling, cardboard-stiff salt cod and cheese of all kinds. Pedestrians are bustling along or ambling more slowly, with straw baskets of vegetables, groceries and loaves of bread peeking out. One or two are window-shopping. A young scooter-rider noses impatiently past.

As one rounds the corner the square comes into view. It's a busy scene. Trestle tables are laid out with a profusion of brightly coloured produce. Scents of fruit and vegetables, fish and meat permeate the air. A small three-wheeler van is piled with wooden produce-crates. Walking between the stalls one sees that in this corner are fresh greens of all kinds. Over there are two women selling just one kind of cheese. Here is a stall heaped with mushrooms. And another with fish and seafood laid out on ice.

Behind that row of stalls is a shopfront with an array of pork products. Next to that is a wine shop with a dark, cave-like interior, and beside that a restaurant and café where morning coffee-drinkers are chatting at outdoor tables, reading their papers or just sitting quietly observing the scene. Further along this side is another restaurant, not yet open but making preparations for the lunch trade as tables are set out by uniformed, aproned waiters. Through a narrow opening next to the café can be glimpsed another street running into the square, with a restaurant sign just discernible in the dim light. Above the hubbub you can see that the buildings that edge the square are similar but

subtly varied: of four, five or six storeys; each layer with its tall windowed balconies overlooking the vitality below.

By mid-afternoon, all the market bustle will be over, the trestles dismantled and the market detritus washed away. The square will rest quietly before the evening eaters and drinkers return after work for a glass of wine at the *enoteca* (wine bar), an evening walk, an *aperitivo* and, perhaps, dinner, focusing on what has been good from the market today. You are in Campo dei Fiori, Rome, at the heart of a gastronomic quarter.

Losing Market-Centred Space

This kind of space is now the exception rather than the rule for most urban dwellers. The decline of gastronomic quarters can be traced through the history of the food market. From pre-Roman times until the early to mid 20th century, food markets and their attendant land uses of food and wine shops and eating places provided a continuous urban function at the centre of urban quarters. Food markets were generally located in the place for ritual, government, feast days and other public ceremonies. Markets were practically and

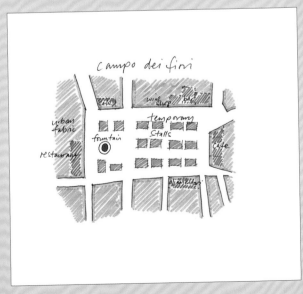

Right
The Campo dei Fiori area in Rome demonstrates a mixed-use building typology at walkable scale around the market. The block typologies are human scaled, with cafés, shops and small business at ground level and apartments above.

symbolically important to the public life of the town. This design typology has been an extraordinarily long-surviving urban presence, a thriving form that attests to the fundamental urban importance of our relationship with food. We have needed food in cities not just to eat to keep alive, but to symbolise our relationship with the town through rituals and feasting at the heart of urban space.

The design rules governing such space gave us fine-grained, mixed land-uses focused on food and drink, and can still help to create convivial city form, but markets and their supporting land uses came close to extinction in many 20th-century cities and towns in Europe. They no longer fitted ideas about what was appropriate for the modern city, either as symbols of civic engagement or as venues for food production, exchange and consumption. From early in the 20th century, transformations of settlement and retailing began to exclude food diversity from cities.

Markets, small shops and city-edge market gardens began to decline. Productive green spaces in cities disappeared. In sharp decline were private vegetable gardens, edge-of-city orchards, fruit trees in streets and a profusion of allotments. By the post-Second World War period, the loss of traditional market halls and outdoor markets, the decline in numbers of allotments in urban areas, and the disappearance of farms and market gardens close to the city tended to be viewed as inevitable

and desirable aspects of modernisation, reaching its apotheosis in the exclusionary zoning patterns of the well-planned city.

Postwar urban redevelopment schemes were on Modernist principles, which meant they were at low densities and car based. They identified markets, their surrounding high-density settlement patterns and proximity to food production, with an outmoded past. Eventually, the advent of supermarkets proved the death knell for many such food-centred spatial patterns across Europe.

All this was perhaps inevitable. Massive increases in the rate and scale of urbanisation marked much of Europe, as it did the rest of the Western world, and meshed nicely with the changing consumption patterns of both suburbia and the more recent conurbation development of the megalopolis in the late 20th century. These changes reflect a particular political economy that has had profound spatial consequences, today reflected in the spread of Euro-sprawl. At the urban conurbation level there has been what Professor Sir Peter Hall calls a spatial resorting in which centripetal forces of urban development have been dominant. Much of the economic and social action now takes place at the edge of town, with food-related urban-fringe activities and land uses largely replaced by low-density housing, business parks, distributions centres, megamalls, and superstore and bulky goods retailing. Many parts of this rapidly expanding megalopolis have no centres based on the public realm, while historic centres have variously declined or become gentrified-living and elite-consumption zones, and sometimes a complex mix of these patterns emerges.

Cities and Food Now

These spatial and economic transformations have tended to reinforce unsustainable and unconvivial approaches to urban development that fit a car-dependent, low-density, monofunctional land-use pattern. As for urban development generally, much of the architectural centre of gravity in food terms is in the urban conurbation, where wholesale-food distribution centres sit on major arterial roads and out-of-town supermarkets are located at the apex of dendritic street patterns. The 'exit ramp architecture' of office parks on the urban fringe is marked by their internalised food spaces where employees eat and socialise in the private realm. The roads that connect these spaces to the traditional city are sites for car-based food consumption from supermarkets, fast-food outlets and 'road pantries' located at service stations.

Within the city, the working population lunches at chain sandwich shops and food courts, while their employers may dine in landmark tall buildings – the icons that architecturally brand the expensive restaurants and private dining spaces that surmount them. Many corner shops have been replaced by supermarket-owned chains selling prepackaged and prepared foods.

Our prevailing food-production model reflects and mirrors these changes to where and how we live, work and eat. In the early 21st century, we primarily rely on intensive, chemically dependent and, now increasingly, genetically modified food production, intensive processing and packaging of food, and long-distance transportation, with enormous wholesaling facilities to serve very large-scale, car-dependent industrialised (and now also 'functional' and 'nutrimedical') food retailing. Food companies seek vertical integration from farm to plate, as far as possible to externalise environmental and social costs. And these costs are substantial, including impoverishing producers, diminishing consumers' tastes, and creating unacceptable food miles and food deserts through profit-maximising spatial practices.

Italian – and now worldwide – initiatives such as Slow Food and Slow Cities have emerged to fight these trends and celebrate the quality and uniqueness of the local and regional. Meanwhile, the growth in interest in fair-trade food, organic food, farmers' markets, local food cooperatives, better school food and food poverty projects is also challenging the largely unacknowledged social, environmental and economic costs of out-of-season, out-of-region food practices from the local to the global scale.

> Architectural discourse seems to revel in the dystopic, fragmented nature of the city of the 21st century both in the centre and on the edge. It is exciting to design an upmarket restaurant behind a hidden door on a dark, dirty street; the contrast between private wealth and public squalor adds to the atmosphere.

As yet, though, architectural and urban design responses to the ways food is both purchased and consumed lag far behind these developments. Architectural discourse seems to revel in the dystopic, fragmented nature of the city of the 21st century both in the centre and on the edge. It is exciting to design an upmarket restaurant behind a hidden door on a dark, dirty street; the contrast between private wealth and public squalor adds to the atmosphere. It does not provoke debate about the loss of an acceptable public realm or the way in which that restaurant could have contributed to that realm. The architect who describes the internal space for eating at a business-park office building or a megamall food court as 'just like a street' is ignoring the real food conditions he or she has been party to creating. The restaurant (or private dining room) at the top of the icon building is there to reinforce the power of those able to afford to dine there. It celebrates inequality and gives nothing back to the street.

Designing the Gastronomic Quarter

By contrast, the notion of the gastronomic quarter is intended to tease out some of the spatial dimensions of more enlightened approaches to food in cities. The quarter can include any or all of the following elements and more: market halls and streets, food stalls, cafés, restaurants, bars and food shops, market gardens, productive street trees and other planting, vegetable gardens and allotments. It is likely to be located in dense urban fabric that mixes land uses at a fine grain and emphasises human scale. It can still be found in many European towns and cities, and examples include

The figure-ground of traditional market-centred space in the style of Camillo Sitte shows how closely the marketplace related to other aspects of civic life – church and state. The figure-ground of Nuremberg shows a series of well-connected 'outdoor rooms' in which buildings front up to streets and squares to contribute to comfortable height-to-width ratios and a pleasing balance between positive and negative space.

Below
Market-focused urban fabric, Granada
Just south of the new Granada market hall, a market-focused urban fabric of human-scaled streets and squares has been renovated, introducing simple new paving, landscaping and street furniture with considerable skill and restraint to enrich the daily food-shopping experience.

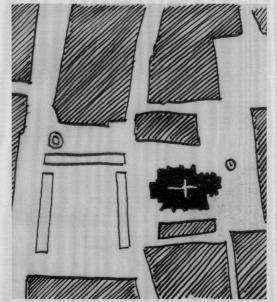

Successful gastronomic quarters tend to exhibit a series of well-configured outdoor rooms – usually urban squares – that demonstrate the appropriate level of enclosure, that is, with height-to-width ratios of built form that are neither too narrow nor too broad, as the figure-ground in the style of Camillo Sitte illustrates.

places that have simply continued for centuries and others that have been revived, revitalised or created from new.

Examples from London, Villeneuve-sur-Lot, Angoulême, Rome and Granada illustrate some of the design approaches that reconnect city design and food relationships for more sustainable, convivial places. With limited space here within which to explore the idea of the gastronomic quarter, the emphasis in this article is on food exchange and consumption within markets and their surrounding areas, but could equally have dealt with the design of the quarter in relation to food production through green space within and on the edge of towns, or with space for 'value adding' processing of produce.

Successful gastronomic quarters tend to exhibit a series of well-configured outdoor rooms – usually urban squares – that demonstrate the appropriate level of enclosure, that is, with height-to-width ratios of built form that are neither too narrow nor too broad, as the figure-ground in the style of Camillo Sitte illustrates. These outdoor rooms act as positive and vital spaces within the urban fabric. The edges of such spaces are three-dimensional and complex, allowing places for people to pause, sit and contemplate the changing scene. These conditions tend to be found in 'traditional' or 'vernacular' townscapes where gastronomic quarters demonstrate a strongly marked sense of place and a good fit between the form of the space and its numerous social, economic and environmental functions. But this does not mean these are nostalgic places, or that other architectural idioms are excluded; simply that new interventions need to demonstrate good manners towards their context.

In Granada, for example, the new market hall, using a Modernist architectural idiom for its built structure, relates sensitively to the surrounding urban fabric.

Above
New market hall, Granada
The market hall uses a
Modernist architectural idiom
for materials and structural
elements whilst relating
sensitively, in terms of
placement, scale and
permeability, to the
surrounding older urban fabric.
Avoiding the temptation to
create an 'object' building, the
new hall provides not only a
new edge to an existing outdoor
room, but has been
strengthened as an urban
element by sensitive
refurbishment, in similar
materials, of well-enclosed,
walkable space around it.

The market hall helps form one side of an enclosed 'outdoor room', an urban square that provides a foreground to the market's facade, yet is more than just an aesthetically pleasing setting for the market. It is an active place used for produce deliveries and market stalls, supported by simple, elegant landscaping and space to sit or promenade.

The market at Testaccio, in a southern quarter of Rome, takes up a city block in an area configured by a strong rectilinear grid of streets. The semicovered market building does not have any architectural distinction, but is a lively and bustling market space in a quarter that demonstrates some useful urban features, including medium to high housing densities and mixed uses, which support a local catchment for the market. The local building typology is fine-grained and generally configured as cafés, shops, offices and small workshops on the ground floors, typically with multiple entrances to three- to eight-storey housing above. Buildings are contiguous on regular city blocks with strong edges, reinforcing enclosure and contributing to good height-to-width ratios in streets abutting the market.

One of the most important qualities for the gastronomic quarter is accessibility. Successful quarters like Testaccio and central Granada have created locations that are walkable for a good proportion of users and encourage access by modes (bicycle, scooter, bus, tram, train and taxi) other than cars. These quarters are also highly permeable and their human scale is further reinforced by an absence of large servicing or delivery vehicles. In both Testaccio

and Granada, the internal connectivity of the quarter is ensured by creating human-scaled walkable areas that relate in density and texture to the surrounding townscape, while external connectivity is increased by good public transport links to the rest of the city.

Market Halls and Structures
Enclosed market structures are not critical to the success of a gastronomic quarter, as Testaccio demonstrates, but there are some famous examples, such as the Mercat de la Boqueria in Barcelona (one of many across Europe) that give great distinction to their area and are rightly world famous. There are also very many less-distinguished but nonetheless attractive buildings that reinforce the market as being at the heart of the quarter. New or renovated market halls developed in places as diverse as Paris (L'Enfant Rouge), Angoulême, London (Borough Market) and Granada (Mercat Municipale) suggest that variations on the market-hall typology are undergoing an architectural and social renaissance.

Where possible, the gastronomic quarter should revitalise existing good-quality buildings and spaces that give opportunities for adaptive reuse related to food. Both new and existing buildings provide opportunities for market traders to personalise their stalls, raising the visual display of fruit, vegetables, meat, fish, cheese and other produce to a rich and sumptuous level – an enduring delight in market spaces. And long-life, loose-fit design principles seem especially suitable for markets. Cardiff market's 19th-century spaces still work well, while Borough Market in the inner south London area of Southwark next to the Thames has been revitalised after a long period of decline as a wholesale market. The latter is located on the site of an ancient open-air market covered over

Above
Covered market, Cardiff, Wales The covered market works as both a place and a fine-grained element in the pedestrian path system. It forms an enclosed, glass-roofed space – a variation on the 'outdoor room' typology – that hides behind the street facade on one side and offers a grand entrance on the other. Although no longer enjoying a profusion of trade in keeping with its architectural grandeur, the market retains some of its fruit-and-vegetable, bakery and meat stalls.

in the 19th century by semienclosed structures of considerable architectural interest and charm. The iron halls, surmounted by sawtooth roofs with extensive skylit areas, are wrapped around and beneath railway bridges, vaults and arches leading into London Bridge station to the east.

As the centrepiece of the gastronomic quarter, the market can be constructed of remarkably flimsy structures. Many food markets successfully rely on basic construction materials where the urban design context is right. In Rome's Campo dei Fiori, and at Trastevere, the market structures are simple stalls that are built and dismantled for each market day. At the centre of each quarter, the daily market of fruit, vegetables, fish and meat is set up on collapsible, portable stalls serviced by small three-wheeler vans that fit the sometimes-medieval streets of the surrounding *centro*. Both these squares, and the local quarters within which they sit, are characterised by dense, medium-rise, mixed-use buildings. In Villeneuve-sur-Lot, basic elements, trestles and umbrellas are easily set up and dismantled while giving a strong structure to the market, which is set in an arcaded *bastide* square that forms a successfully enclosed outdoor room.

Catchments: Niche or Nostalgia?

Catchment issues are important but can be complex, as Borough Market demonstrates. In recent years, while its wholesaling function has dwindled, new vitality has been introduced through a farmers' market that has become increasingly popular. There is a growing selection of organic meat, fish, dairy produce, bread, fruit and vegetables, plants, grocery items and wine on sale. The market supports not only a local catchment of residents but a number of other users from the wider London region, as well as visitors from elsewhere.

As at Campo dei Fiori in Rome, Borough's catchment represents a community of interest as well as a geographical community. Residential development to the south includes modern estates of poor quality, housing a predominantly low-income population. The advent of the market is seen by some here as an aspect of unwelcome gentrification. Its very success is cited as a factor rapidly pushing up house prices in the Borough area and squeezing out traditional communities who could not in any case afford the high prices at the farmers' market. In a context of 'cheap' industrialised food whose externalities are unacknowledged in deleterious environmental or health terms, good-quality market produce is perceived as a luxury commodity, not a right for all. It is tempting to speculate that the growth of successful gastronomic quarters does contribute to gentrification, but the results of these food processes in city space are as yet underresearched, so definitive answers about the positive and negative effects cannot yet be provided.

Borough Market and Campo dei Fiori also attract one of the main criticisms levelled at high-quality markets; that they are gastronomic tourism zones trading on nostalgia about a lost way of life and pandering to the obsessions of wealthy food-literate tourists. It is certainly true that these markets are attractive to affluent tourists. Borough has drawn them to a previously obscure location while the Campo, in the centre of historic Rome, draws a global community of interest yet is also clearly a much-loved local centre. Trastevere, meanwhile, serves a much more local-only population, yet the urban structure in which it sits is remarkably similar to other sites explored here, so its vitality cannot be ascribed to tourism alone.

Catchment issues are closely tied to those of scale, with the gastronomic quarter needing to support small local shops and eating places that are well designed and located for surrounding communities. The range of food-related activities contributes to the quarter's vitality. In and around Campo dei Fiori, at Trastevere and in Testaccio there is a rich selection of individually owned food shops, cafés and bars that both connect with and support the main market. In each case, the daily market helps to support these ancillary land-uses of grocery shops, wine merchants, bakeries, restaurants, bars and cafés on ground floors with offices and housing above. The Testaccio area supports one of Rome's best food shops, Volpetti, on nearby Via Marmorata. At Campo dei Fiori local food shops include the famous Antica Norcineria Viola devoted to pork products. The land-use mix is always highly diverse and fine-grained.

The gastronomic quarter should provide for servicing, including deliveries and waste removal at ground level, by small vehicles rather than large trucks. At Campo dei Fiori, produce is brought into the square by small vehicles. These neither undercut the pedestrian-friendly atmosphere nor disrupt frontages needed for the enclosure of the space in the way that larger trucks do when servicing areas. Boxes on the back of very small vans add to the lively atmosphere and also reflect the predominance of small-scale producers and retailers, historically a characteristic of markets, and implying a fine grain of land use.

All these elements together allow local people to walk, cycle or scooter from home or work daily to enjoy the sensual experience of the market, to buy produce and to socialise. Very fresh food – emphasising season and region – is bought in small amounts that are light enough to carry the short distance home.

Conclusion

Sensitive design can contribute to a convivial food-oriented urban fabric. This is an evolving urban pattern, yet one that draws on long-term, time-tested design arrangements to support rich social relationships centred on growing, transporting, buying, cooking and eating good food.

Design research suggests that traditional cities implicitly understood these relationships, creating workable and sometimes uplifting public market spaces, while Modernist-inspired exclusionary zoning undermines public space and the fine grain of functions that go with it. Food production on the edges of cities, food exchange at markets and food consumption within the built fabric that surrounds markets were once spatially configured at a human scale. These spatial arrangements were accompanied by opportunities for social interaction and conviviality centred on food, allowing for social ritual and maintaining a sense of community. They avoided the sterile, alienating and unhealthy conditions we now suffer from in much food growing, retailing and eating. The gastronomic quarters that have been surveyed here show some of the necessary design qualities that could be retrieved or built in city space to overcome such dystopic urban environments.

It is possible to combat unconvivial trends in spatial design. Various architectural and design typologies can be employed to create workable public spaces, centred on nodes of intensity of activity around food, that are human scaled, mixed use, fine-grained and diverse. For sustainability and for pleasure, this should be the way forward. ∆

David Bell

David Bell teaches cultural studies at Manchester Metropolitan University. He has diverse research interests, including sexual identities and cultures, science and technology, consumption and cultural policy. His recent books include *The Sexual Citizen: Queer Politics and Beyond* (with Jon Binnie); *Cyberculture: The Key Concepts* (with Brian Loader, Nicholas Please and Doug Schuler); and *City of Quarters* (with Mark Jayne). He is currently co-editing two volumes on lifestyle media, and writing a book on science, technology and culture.

Jon Binnie

Jon Binnie is senior lecturer in human geography at Manchester Metropolitan University. His interests focus on sexualised urban space, particularly in a transnational context, as well as the spatial politics of cosmopolitanism, citizenship and everyday life. He is the author of *The Globalization of Sexuality* (Sage, 2004) and co-author of *The Sexual Citizen: Queer Politics and Beyond* (Polity, 2000) and *Pleasure Zones: Bodies, Cities, Spaces* (Syracuse University Press, 2001). He is currently jointly editing a volume of essays on cosmopolitan urbanism due to published by Routledge in 2005.

Louisa Carter

Louisa Carter is a doctoral student in the Departments of Architecture and Planning at the University of Queensland, Brisbane. In her research on issues of governance, space and leisure practice, she seeks to provide empirical spatial evidence for cultural theory. Louisa has degrees in architecture and arts from the University of Queensland. She has worked for over 10 years in the development industry and local government in southeast Queensland as an architect and urban planner. Currently she is an urban development strategist, providing cross-disciplinary advice in urban renewal, transport policy and knowledge services.

Jeffrey W Cody

Jeffrey Cody, professor in the Department of Architecture at the Chinese University of Hong Kong, has taught architectural history there since 1995. He is the author of *Building in China: Henry K Murphy's 'Adaptive' Architecture, 1914–1935* (University of Washington Press, 2001) and *Exporting American Architecture, 1870–2000* (Routledge, 2003). He is currently working as a senior project specialist at the Getty Conservation Institute, Los Angeles.

Mary C Day

Mary Day has been a technical writer for the School of Nursing of the Hong Kong Polytechnic University since 2001. A Hong Kong resident for nine years and trained as a nutritionist, she co-edited *The Globalization of Chinese Food* (University of Hawaii Press, 2002). Since 1976, Jeffrey Cody and Mary Day have travelled extensively outside the US, sharing an abiding interest in finding affordable, delicious food everywhere they have visited.

Gil Doron

Gil Doron is a senior lecturer at the University of Brighton School of Architecture and Design. Hus doctorate research, 'The Dead Zone and the Architecture of Transgression', is due for completion at the Bartlett School of Architecture, UCL. He has taught design and history and theory of architecture at various universities in London, and has published articles in numerous journals, such as *Δ*, *Archis*, *City* and *Loud Paper*. He is a freelance curator and the founder of www.transgressivearchitecture.org, which works on the issue of inclusive public space through art and design.

Nisha Fernando

Nisha Fernando is assistant professor of interior architecture at the University of Wisconsin-Stevens Point, and a doctoral candidate in architecture at the University of Wisconsin-Milwaukee. Her dissertation examines the influence of culture on urban street use, with a focus on Chinatown, New York City. Trained as an architect in Sri Lanka, she was involved in many residential and urban design projects there. Her research interests extend to culture–environment aspects in design, flexibility in public spaces and qualitative methodology in environmental design.

Karen A Franck

Karen A Franck is a professor in the New Jersey School of Architecture and the Department of Humanities at the New Jersey Institute of Technology, where she also serves as director of the PhD Program in Urban Systems. She has a PhD in environmental psychology from the City University of New York. Her interest in design and its influence on everyday life has resulted in several books, including *New Households, New Housing* (Van Nostrand Reinhold, 1989), *Ordering Space* (Van Nostrand Reinhold, 1994) and *Architecture Inside Out* (Wiley-Academy, 2000). She guest-edited *Δ*'s first issue devoted to food – 'Food and Architecture' (2002).

Rachel Hurst

Rachel Hurst is a senior lecturer and design studio coordinator for the architecture programme at the University of South Australia. She studied at the South Australian Institute of Technology, spent 15 years in practice and was a founding partner of LUXE Design. Her collaborative research practice with Jane Lawrence uses food as an analogy and frame of reference for teaching design. In addition to writing regularly for design journals and researching contemporary Australian Modernism, she curated the inaugural Architecture Symposium for the 2004 Adelaide Festival of Arts, based on food and architecture.

Jane Lawrence

Jane Lawrence is a senior lecturer and design studio coordinator for the interior architecture programme at the University of South Australia. Since graduating from the South Australian Institute of Technology, she has continued professional practice through consultancy projects. She has received numerous research grants and, with colleague Rachel Hurst, has been awarded three teaching awards for innovation and excellence. Their mutual interests in the everyday underpin their collaborative artworks, which have been exhibited in national and international exhibitions and publications, most recently in *Eating Architecture* (MIT Press, 2004).

Brian McGrath

Brian McGrath, architect and urban designer, is co-founder of urban-interface, a collaborative group exploring the intersection of emerging paradigms in urban ecology and design incorporating new spatial analysis technologies. A co-investigator in the Baltimore Ecosystem Study, he also teaches at Columbia and New School universities in New York, and Chulalongkorn University in Bangkok. His online project, Manhattan Timeformations, has received international recognition. He is co-editing a forthcoming issue of *Δ* on the impact of remote sensing and telecommunication technologies on the future of the city.

Susan Parham

Susan Parham has written on food and cities for many years. Her research centres on the relationship between food and sustainable, convivial cities, and includes analysis of the design of all kinds of domestic and urban spaces. With a background in political economy, town planning and urban design, she is currently a PhD candidate in the cities programme at the London School of Economics and Political Science, where she is writing on design typologies in support of convivial cities. Susan is a director of CAG Consultants, an urban regeneration consultancy based in the UK, and chair of the Council for European Urbanism.

Gail Satler

Gail Satler is professor of sociology at Hofstra University and Cooper Union. She received her doctorate in sociology from the City University of New York. Her research focuses on the intersections between urban, architectural, sociological and aesthetic theory. Writings include *Frank Lloyd Wright's Living Space* (Northern Illinois University Press, 1999) and a forthcoming book on recent architectural and sociological trends in Chicago entitled *Two Tales of a City: Architecture and Sociology in Chicago 1986–2004* (Northern Illinois University Press). Other publications explore New York City restaurants and the global economy.

Masaaki Takahashi

Masaaki Takahashi is a Tokyo-based independent design journalist writing for various international publications. His recent book, *Design City Tokyo* (Wiley-Academy, 2004), covers high-end design and the intriguing lifestyle of Tokyoites. He also contributed to *Tokyo Architecture & Design* (TeNues, 2004), writing on new urban development, and is now working on a similar guide book for Spanish publisher Loft publications.

Danai Thaitakoo

Danai Thaitakoo is a lecturer in the Department of Landscape Architecture, Chulalongkorn University, Bangkok. He received a bachelor's degree in landscape architecture from Chulalongkorn, a masters in landscape architecture from Harvard and a PhD in environmental planning from the University of California at Berkeley. His research interest is in the field of landscape ecology, with an emphasis on the application of landscape spatial structure analysis and modelling to landscape planning and design. *Δ*

Shopping at MoMA

Anticipating last autumn's relaunch at the Museum of Modern Art (MoMA) in Manhattan, Gluckman Mayner Architects helped to reconceive a key moneymaker, notes Craig Kellogg.

Patrons in slow motion murmur aesthetic judgements, and a silly amount of money changes hands. But this is not Sir Norman Foster's year-old Asprey flagship, a Modernist temple to luxury shopping in Manhattan's Trump Tower. Not exactly. This is around the corner and down the street, inside architect Yoshio Tanaguchi's spectacularly expanded Museum of Modern Art (MoMA), where general admission now costs $20. MoMA doesn't show diamonds as Asprey does. Then again, the museum was not exactly founded, in 1929, to send visitors home with expensive souvenirs. In fact, a full decade passed before MoMA even became a retailer, in 1939.

Today even Rem Koolhaas shops here, apparently. A-list museums like MoMA attract the very same people who frequent the adjacent stretch of Fifth Avenue dominated by luxury-brand flagships. Good thing a lazy afternoon spent looking at art is not incompatible, or even all that different, from the quest for a new purse at Prada. Because the expanded MoMA must sell more

Bottom left
MoMA's wall of windows offers panoramic city views unusual in retail environments.

Bottom right
Gluckman Mayner's casework details help structure and organise tableware displayed
in the ground-floor design shop.

Top right
A metal storage system in the reading room provides
for book display as well as conventional shelving.

posters than ever before to keep the museum's acres of new
plasterboard in fresh white paint.

Everything about the revamped museum feels expensive
and oversized, like a Hummer sport utility truck. *Architectural
Record* critic Suzanne Stephens compared the sight of Claude
Monet's 42-foot-long *Reflections of Clouds on the Water-Lily
Pond* in the gigantic new MoMA atrium to 'a shower curtain
tacked up on a wall', while *New Yorker* art critic Peter Scheldahl
said that the installation turned the Monet into 'a big, soiled Band-
Aid'. Adrift on a very large white wall, it is not the only painting
that once filled a gallery at the old museum absolutely to the
brim – before the remodelling – and now looks like a lonely
gift-shop poster hanging in a bachelor's studio apartment.

Today, MoMA sells small poster-sized reproductions of
Water Lilies for $17.95, along with trinkets and more expensive
souvenirs. There was once a jumbo retail shop in the museum
proper, as well as one across the street that was completely
updated several years ago by 1100 Architect. (The same firm
was also responsible for designing the satellite MoMA
shopfront in SoHo.) Taniguchi's plans called for replacing the
shop in the old museum building with a bar and restaurant,
so MoMA hired Richard Gluckman, of Gluckman Mayner
Architects, to outfit new facilities in Taniguchi's addition. The
new space, though not terribly larger than the abandoned
shop, is broken into three distinct boutiques on separate levels.
Two of the three are inside the museum proper, past the
ticket-takers. Although Gluckman Mayner did not design the
small one on the top floor, the firm was given free rein with
the other – a 'reading room' shop meant to resemble an art
library – across a second-floor bridge from Taniguchi's atrium.

Gluckman was an obvious choice, having developed
galleries for the Andy Warhol Museum and high-concept retail
for the likes of Helmut Lang. Boxy, freestanding cabinetry in
Gluckman's reading room evokes the deeply rational layout
of casework in Lang's SoHo boutique. The assembled
catalogues and monographs at MoMA are shelved and
displayed in stacked metal boxes that would do Donald Judd
proud. Illumination comes from recessed ceiling spotlights
and a wall of windows overlooking 54th Street. Stretching
almost the length of the space is an impressive refectory table
that invites visitors to start reading even before they hand
over their charge cards. Salespeople, not docents or librarians,
monitor the exit.

Top left
An axial view through MoMA's new ground-floor design shop, also by Gluckman Mayner, centres on an enlarged silhouette of the 1948 La Chaise lounger by Charles and Ray Eames.

Bottom left
Typical fixtures deployed in multiples establishe a rhythm for the ground-floor shop plan.

Top right
The long counter built of solid surfacing incorporates displays and supplemental cash registers in the ground-floor shop.

MoMA Retail sells mass-produced modern objects collected by the museum and further blurs boundaries with museum-like displays.

Gluckman Mayner's strictly controlled architectural palette includes wood with a clear finish and wall panels of cement board.

Gluckman Mayner was also responsible for a new ground-floor shop, which feels a lot more like a traditional museum book store by default. The little bins of gaily coloured pencils and tricked-out plastic pens in crinkly cellophane wrap had to go somewhere. There are also tableware, picture books and Modernist knickknacks, of course, along with the dreaded posters. But the architectural palette of cement-board, metal-mesh curtains and terrazzo toughens the space, as do Gluckman's experiments with unexpected mutant materials such as violently freckled greenish rubber for the poster bins, and indestructible solid-plastic counter surfacing that's otherwise used for kitchens.

One Manhattan retailer who has an admitted fetish for such counter tops is Murray Moss. His celebrated retail gallery,

Moss, remains a haunt for people who care desperately about design. In Tanaguchi's MoMA galleries devoted to industrial design, the sleek vitrines are reminiscent of the museum-like glass cases in the tableware department at Moss. Who inspired whom? I found myself peering in at the museum's unusual bottle-green Alvar Aalto vase, wondering where I could buy one. After striking out on Ebay and Google, I discovered that mass-produced versions were available online from the MoMA Retail website. Assuming, that is, I would settle for clear glass. It was life imitating art, imitating design ... on just too many levels, frankly. But as the *New York Times* noted recently with a quip attributed to Andy Warhol, eventually 'all museums will become department stores'. ⚙+

Below
Simple materials imaginatively used
create a range of extraordinary effects.

Fawood Children's Centre

Below
Simple materials imaginatively used
create a range of extraordinary effects.

Jeremy Melvin visits the Fawood Children's Centre on the Stonebridge Estate in northwest London and discovers how Alsop and Partners have creatively worked within the bounds of policy to produce a building with an exhilarating choice of recycled materials that gives children back the freedom to play in an exciting environment without wrapping them up in cotton wool.

Below left and right
Over the next couple of years, the Fawood Children's Centre's
context will be transformed out of all recognition, symbolically
putting children at the centre of the regenerated community.

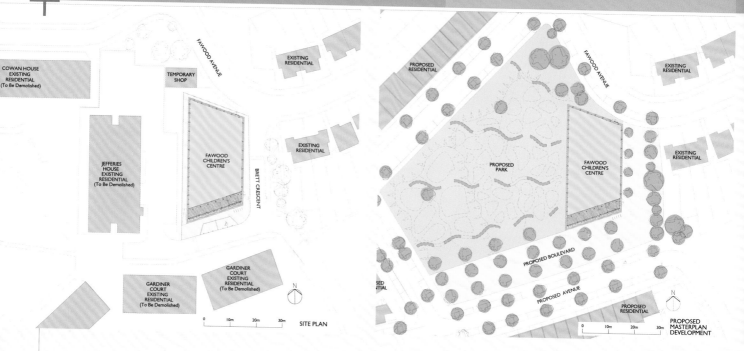

SITE PLAN

PROPOSED
MASTERPLAN
DEVELOPMENT

Shipping containers, steel mesh and the first Mongolian yurt to comply fully with the UK's newly onerous regulations on energy efficiency may not be the items that most designers would select for a children's centre. But then, what would be? Most environments for children depend on clichéd imagery and tokens to reflect their function. Apart from low-level windows and WCs, architecture, unlike politics or psychology, has few conventions for dealing with childhood; and this, within a highly specific context, is precisely what Will Alsop's Fawood Children's' Centre seeks to challenge.

That context is both political and physical. Britain's politicians have finally realised that kissing babies does not ensure their lifelong support, and still less does it ingrain a lasting sense of social responsibility. Meld those abstract perceptions into the physical context of the Stonebridge Estate in Harlesden, northwest London, one of the capital's most deprived areas, and you have a spur to do something dramatic. Despite 10 years of work by the Stonebridge Housing Action Trust, its dystopian, 16-storey concrete slabs, fragmented and ill-defined public spaces, unclear desire lines and movement patterns speak eloquently of the fractures in its social fabric, its deprivation and lack of opportunity. If the government is to implement its much-vaunted 'family-friendly policies' under the Sure Start initiative, Stonebridge is a good place to start.

The centre's galvanised-steel frame and polycarbonate roof provides a covered and secure enclosure, with the shipping containers and yurt offering fully serviced interiors. Children move easily between inside and outside, enriching the curriculum that government has determined for them with possibilities for play and social interaction. As the centre's head, Sarah Neno, confirms, a flexible and imaginative building is a very good way of finding imaginative ways of interpreting educational prescriptions. In all there are free places for

35 three- and four-year-olds, paid places for a rather smaller number of twos and threes, plus a unit for severely autistic children as well as offices for staff working on outreach family support initiatives, and a small conference suite for training. The idea is to combine all the services orientated towards children, from childcare and play through preschool education to family support, in one location. It promises much for the local community, but the architectural challenge is how to give concrete expression to worthy abstract intentions.

Childhood here rarely follows the images beloved by advertisers and retailers, so a conventional crèche designed in an idiom derived from such clichés would be meaningless. The existing context suggests a gritty social realism that might come out well in art-house movies, but is hardly likely to inculcate a sense of citizenship in preschools. As the first phases of the overall estate redevelopment unfold, they seem to subscribe to that polite Modernism of steel frames, white rendered walls, flat roofs and large windows: infinitely preferable to the po-mo coloured-brick-and-pitched-roofs of 1980s' 'community architecture', its proportional systems and subtle reference to minimalism are probably lost on under-fives.

Alsop eschews these inferences of architecture as a means of social control or a private system of esoteric knowledge. His evolving creative practice strives to bring individual perceptions and aspirations into contact with policy. This brand of what he is happy, at least on occasion, to call 'community architecture', is based around active participation in creative exercises rather than passive 'consultation' where questions often presuppose their answers. It also has a trace

Top
Evening sun plays with the coloured lozenges and
casts shadows with the flower-petal-like 'rosettes'.

Bottom
East elevation: the lozenges interweave with the mesh. Eventually the
perimeter planting will grow to cover the strip of mesh below.

of roots in art practice, owing at least something to
Pop Art in its fascination with finding the potential for
expression in the everyday and commonplace. Alsop
does not simulate a faux childhood with fluffy bunnies
and crude cartoons: instead, his approach encourages
an idiom to emerge from the interaction between
communal hopes and the opportunities policy might
offer within a framework of creative activity.

With his major urban-regeneration commissions
in Britain's run-down northern industrial cities, the
implications of this approach go far wider than the
remit of one children's centre on a north London
estate. Yet it is a powerful enough statement on its
own. The materials and components, despite their
industrial origins, have a sense of familiarity that is
delightfully denied. The steel frame might have found
its way into a warehouse on the nearby North Circular
Road, but in that location it would not be graced on its
long sides with coloured 'lozenges' and on the short
with scrunched-up pieces of wire mesh that simulate
giant flowers. Nor would a factory have a zone of
planting on either side of its perimeter wall. And
everyone will have seen shipping containers, but rarely
have considered playing or working in them, still less
upending them to make stair or lift towers. But they
lend themselves well to such uses. Of necessity robust
and flexible, these qualities make them adaptable to
more than the backs of pantechnicons, or the decks
of cargo carriers. With structure only along the edges,
they can be knocked together to make wider spaces

If you liked this article and want to know more about spaces for young children, from nurseries to museums, from hotels to play-rooms, you might be interested in *Interiors for Under 5s*, by Melissa Jones (Wiley-Academy, 2005), available in hardback (ISBN 0470093323) at £34.99, from www.wiley.com

than single units, and provided you don't go too close to an edge, or remove too much of the corrugation, openings can be punched into their sides for windows. And, of course, they can be painted any colour.

As well as reconstituting the relationship between policy, architecture and user, the design suggests new relationships between indoor and outdoor space, form and function, and even allocation of budget. Just as generous outdoor space means indoor areas can be tighter, so making use of cheap materials and mass-produced containers frees up funds for other purposes. The climate penetrates the steel mesh on the perimeter wall, the mesh managing the useful trick of appearing more transparent from inside than out. As the roof keeps rain out, children can be 'outside', but safe and secure much of the time. All they need are their jackets. Children can centre their activity where they want in areas which, thanks to Alsops and the project artist Joanna Turner, are coded by light, atmosphere and texture rather than the conventions associated with particular activities. After all, it matters little whether they learn the alphabet with their feet in a sandpit or sitting in serried, cross-legged ranks in

front of a blackboard. And if the children do get cold, they can
retreat into the yurt. It has a traditional lattice-wall structure
and radial rafters, but also two layers of canvas separated
by lamb's-wool insulation and double-glazed windows –
options that don't seem to have been necessary in the vastly
less clement climate of the Asian steppes.

Over the next couple of years, the centre's immediate
surroundings will be transformed beyond all recognition. The
overbearing concrete slabs will go and leave a park in
their wake. Yet even in the present hostile environment,
the design of the building, its large volume mitigated by
subtle colours and gauzy, semitransparent mesh, brings
the promise of future delight. That's not a bad metaphor
for a children's centre, proving that, after all, shipping
containers, Part L compliant yurts and steel mesh
might just add up to a new image for childcare. Δ+

The London Stone Show 2005

The London Stone Show 2005 opened its doors to the world of stone on 5 April.

With more than 140 world-class companies showcasing products of the highest quality, the show attracted thousands of visitors over the three days. Exhibitors from more than 20 countries came to the London Stone Show, the exhibition that is now synonymous with quality.

As well as suppliers and producers of stone, the exhibitors included diamond tool suppliers, stone treatment suppliers and water jet cutters, providing visitors with the opportunity to source and learn about the new and innovative products now available to the industry, all under one roof.

Being the only niche specialist show of its type in the UK, the London Stone Show attracted architects, interior designers, wholesalers, buyers, surveyors, landscapers, property professionals and contractors, as well as a whole host of associated specialists who use natural stone and ancillary products in their work.

The show was opened by Tim Quick of Halpern Architecture, who provided an insight into the world of natural stone and discussed the use of stone in the building industry throughout the UK in recent years, leading the way for many architects and specifiers to discuss their projects with the exhibitors.

Exhibitors at the show were reporting that they had sold products and signed up orders at the show, and had gained plenty of contacts and leads from the high quality and informed visitors.

Johnsons Wellfield Quarries is a family-owned business supplying locally quarried high-quality natural stone products to the UK construction industry in addition to achieving success in exporting materials to both Europe and North America.

Johnsons has long enjoyed a reputation for professional management in supplying high-specification projects in addition to a pedigree reaching back over 150 years. Indeed, many a fine Victorian building bears testimony to the workmanship, superb weathering properties and outstanding natural beauty of the company's stones.

Most recently, Johnsons Wellfields won the contract to supply the prestigious Victoria and Albert museum. If the feedback that Johnsons Wellfields received on its stand at the London Stone Show can be used as an indication, the company has every reason to look forward to continued success in the future.

Stone Systems was launched at the London Stone Show where the firm's theme displayed sandstone products and flooring slate. Although the company deals with most stones from the Indian subcontinent and China, it felt that there was a need for worked sandstone. Vases, urns and pots were displayed along with benches and garden artefacts in both traditional and contemporary design. The firm prides itself on being able to supply bespoke sandstone products ranging from exterior ballustrading to indoor fireplaces and almost anything in-between in a variety of colours. 'We have had a very successful time exhibiting at the London Stone Show, which has proved itself to be the ideal launch pad and has provided us with extremely high-quality leads,' said Stone Systems' sales director Ricky Bedesha.

Mark Palmer, managing director of the London Stone Show, was very pleased with the feedback from both visitors and exhibitors. 'Our aim is to provide the market with a high-quality show that brings a wealth of knowledge to the UK market place, and we have achieved exactly that. Visitors have been able to source from the most spectacular range of high-quality and beautiful products over the three days, and exhibitors have been able to increase their market presence in one of the world's most important markets.'

Mark Palmer was also pleased to announce the launch dates of the Scottish Stone Show 2005 and the Dublin Stone Show 2005, plus the dates of the London Stone Show 2006. 'I am delighted that we are launching the show in Scotland in November this year. With the three shows we can provide the building industry with the ideal forums for meeting new suppliers and customers to continually meet the demands of this growing industry sector.'

For further information on the three shows, please visit www.thestoneshow.com, or contact +44 (0)1442 828173. ᴅ+

Below
One of the bedrooms overlooks the adjacent railway
embankment. Double-glazing units will help cut
down the noise, however the view onto the verdant
embankment and its wildlife is an interesting one.

Self-Build
Housing in
Peckham

Bruce Stewart discovers the whys
and wherefores of self-build for
both architects and occupiers at a
new development in south London.

Below left
The master bedroom looks over the south-facing garden,
although the windows were installed upside down!

Below right
The virtually solid north wall shields the houses from
the noise coming from the nearby railway line.

Tucked behind an ordinary street in south London, a new self-build housing development has recently been completed. The small terrace of houses was built under the supervision of Habitat for Humanity, a US-based charity which has had a presence in the UK since 1995, with varying degrees of success for its projects. However, it is hoped that this new scheme will raise the charity's profile and also reawaken people to the possibilities that self-build can provide for low-income families.

Founded in 1976, the charity is based around the idea of Christian ministry and aims to provide 'a simple, decent place to live'[1] for low-income families. With a down payment and interest-free monthly mortgage repayments, those who could previously not easily afford their own home can now do so. The main commitment that each family must contribute is 'sweat equity' – an investment of a minimum of 500 hours of labour on their own home. To date, the presence of high-profile supporters such as President Carter and Oprah Winfrey has enabled the charity to build over 175,000 homes in more than 3,000 communities worldwide, including places such as Zaire, Malaysia, India, South America and now the UK.

The scheme at Gordon Road, Peckham, was built not only by the intended new owners but with the labour of the staff of some of the biggest corporate institutions in the City. Providing both significant funding and releasing their staff for extended periods of time as a team-building exercise has meant that there was always a reasonable pool of labour to enable the scheme to progress without too many real stoppages. The charity also receives 'gifts in kind' from many construction-industry companies such as Wates, Rockwall and Lafarge, and all white goods are donated by Whirlpool. However, because the houses are being built by an unskilled labour force, training on the job is the only means of getting the work done. Key staff, such as the site manager, carpenter and construction manager, are employed by the charity to oversee the progress of the development, with other skilled tradespeople volunteering their time and expertise to train up the nonskilled volunteers. The mix of high-flying City employees and low-income families trying to get a

Top
Although self-build has a traditionally 'rustic' image, this
development has a contemporary feel, which could help to
make the future of this type of construction more popular.

Bottom
The large monopitch roof was originally intended to incorporate
photovoltaic cells (solar panels). Unfortunately, the panels were
not included in the finished houses.

Overall, this is a good small housing development that avoids the clichés of self-build as it looks contemporary and not like a highly evolved garden shed, the standard of the finishes is reasonable and the space standards good. It is only where the site manager and the architect had slight differences of opinion that any slippage occurs, with the pragmatism of a builder in minor discord with the vision and perfectionism of an architect.

decent home is seen by the charity as one of the key elements to its success. This mix of social strata gives those on low incomes a much-needed confidence boost and empowers them to think beyond their usual expectations.

Unfortunately, until now the selection process of the prospective new residents has been rather haphazard, with individuals responding to adverts in local papers. This approach has meant that in some cases people come on board who are not fully committed, or who don't grasp the idea of a minimum of 500 hours' labour on the site, and end up abandoning the project well before completion. Although the charity works outside the usual role of a housing association or local authority (and as such is not subject to the rigorous planning requirements of such institutions), there is now a move in Southwark for the charity and the local authority to work together. This partnership, it is hoped, will give those on the borough's housing waiting list the opportunity to participate in the self-build schemes as and when they are available. The criteria for eligibility is that applicants are in employment but with a low income (ceiling of £17,000), are in need of housing and live in the borough. As mentioned, the charity is based on the principles of Christian ministry, though there is no religious discrimination in the selection of possible candidates, with existing residents covering a broad range of beliefs.

The site itself is squeezed in between an earlier Habitat for Humanity development and a railway embankment, thus creating several problems from the outset. With the railway line to the north there was a need to buffer noise, therefore the scheme set out to create private south-facing gardens with an almost solid wall facing the embankment. Sustainability is also very much part of the charity's remit, and the incorporation of solar panels and a rainwater harvesting system were therefore important factors in generating the final form of the buildings. However, these ecological elements did not actually make it into the finished buildings, due to several factors, not least of which was funding, though the houses do now have a large, south-facing monopitch roof that can be utilised for photovoltaic cells in the future.

The construction system itself needed to acknowledge the fact that the vast majority of the work would be undertaken by a labour force with absolutely no building experience. From the very first design meetings it was recognised that a very straightforward plan was the only solution, and one of the primary decisions was to ensure that all the angles (where walls met and so on) were to be 90°, thus reducing the margin of error in erecting the shell and internal layout. Another key decision was to reduce the amount of 'wet' trades, such as concreting, bricklaying and plastering, throughout the building process – very much in keeping with the philosophy of the godfather of self-build Walter Segal.[2] Therefore, a timber-frame system with timber cladding was chosen as the most efficient method of erecting the buildings with an unskilled labour force. Interestingly, it is in a project such as this that internal finishing elements have regained their original purpose: for example, skirting boards and cornicing are used as they were when first introduced to the architectural vocabulary as a means of concealing uneven joints between walls and floors or ceilings.

The finished houses are spatially generous with the accommodation consisting of a large open-plan kitchen/living space, two bedrooms and a bathroom on the first floor, and a third bedroom on the second floor. The third bedroom was originally intended as a roof space that could be developed later by the resident family. However, the site manager, Alan Wellington, decided that since the labour and materials were already there it made much more sense to develop the space as part of the initial build rather than residents developing the space at a later date at their own expense. This has worked reasonably well, but the fire door leading up to the third bedroom does cause some difficulties on the first-floor landing and, although there is plenty of light from the donated Velux rooflights, they are awkwardly placed and provide views of the sky only.

There were several other small, but to the architect (Richard Asbury, then working at Burrell Foley Fisher) disappointing, decisions that were made on the spot without his consultation. As his was a completely voluntary role, he was not able to visit the site as often as he would have liked, and therefore had little control over some of the design issues. For example, alongside the less-than-perfect completion of the roof space is the fact that the bedroom windows have been installed upside down, therefore greatly reducing the views out of the room onto the garden. However, the prospective residents did not notice this flaw, and were actually quite happy as it gave

them another usable wall ('We can put the bed against that wall,'[3] was the comment from one new owner).

According to the architect, this was a major learning curve in how to adjust one's expectations from a professional build to the lower, yet still satisfactory (in terms of the planning officer and so on) standards of self-build. As with any building project, there was a time schedule and even with a relatively straightforward construction process delays to the project were inevitable, with the allocation of work taking place on a daily basis depending on how many volunteers were there that day and how long they had been on the site to gain some basic knowledge.

Overall, this is a good small housing development that avoids the clichés of self-build as it looks contemporary and not like a highly evolved garden shed, the standard of the finishes is reasonable and the space standards good. It is only where the site manager and the architect had slight differences of opinion that any slippage occurs, with the pragmatism of a builder in minor discord with the vision and perfectionism of an architect. However, as outlined above, the main concern of the charity is to provide 'a simple decent place to live' – and this development does just that. In fact, for a construction cost of £70,000, equal to the interest-free mortgage of the new residents, they have gained properties valued at £250,000. Not bad for a first home. △+

GORDON ST. PECKHAM	G 0-29%	F 30-39%	E 40%	D 41-49%	C 50-59%	B 60-69%	A 70-100%
QUALITATIVE							
Space-Interior					C		
Space-Exterior						B	
Location				D			
Community						B	
QUANTITATIVE							
Construction Cost						B	
Cost-rental/purchase							A
Cost in use				D			
Sustainability				D			
AESTHETICS							
Good Design?						B	
Appeal					C		
Innovative?				D			

This table is based on an analytical method of success in contributing to a solution to housing need. The criteria are: Quality of life – does the project maintain or improve good basic standards? Quantitative factors – has the budget achieved the best it can? Aesthetics – does the building work visually?

Notes
1 Millard Fuller, *The Building Realisation of Habitat for Humanity: A Simple, Decent Place to Live*, World Publishing (Dallas), 1995.
2 Colin Ward, 'Walter Segal – Community Architect', www.sealselfbuild.co.uk.
3 In conversation with Richard Asbury.

' Bruce Stewart, with Jane Briginshaw, is currently researching and writing *The Architects' Navigation Guide to New Housing*, to be published in autumn 2005 by Wiley-Academy. Bruce Stewart trained as an architect and is currently a college teacher at the Bartlett School of Architecture, UCL London.

McLean's Nuggets

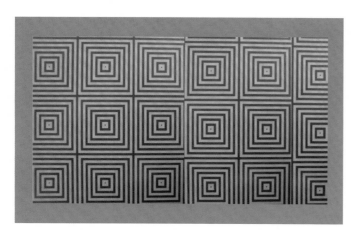

Tranquillity

In our interconnected media-rich world of data (and occasional) information, there has appeared a new market for products, services and research projects that protect and shield us from this social noise. Technologies include Noise or Phase cancellation from Noise Eater, the company that sold us the idea of Buying Quiet, and bespoke 'stealth' wallpapers from defence firm QinetiQ, which uses the Frequency Selective Surface (FSS) of its electrolytically grown wallpapers to 'protect' Wi-Fi networks and delineate Quiet Zones free from the polyphonic chirrup of the mobile phone. In Denmark, 'comfort guru' Dr P Ole Fanger continues his research investigating the impact of the indoor environment on human productivity, comfort and health at the new International Centre for Indoor Environment and Energy at the Danish Technical University. The research examines the relationship between air quality, lighting, physical disposition, thermal comfort, acoustics and your physical state of arousal, in this case specifically in relation to work rate. Initial findings suggest that 'personalised ventilation', where '... different indoor environmental factors can be delegated to the individual', increases comfort and thus productivity, and may also limit energy consumption. Dr Fanger's doctoral thesis 'Thermal Comfort' has sold 13,000 copies. Meanwhile, in Japan, the Pleasant Sleep Consortium, founded at the end of 2003 by nine companies including Matsushita Electric Industrial Co Ltd and Kao Corp, has begun to release product details. The Sleep Room for insomniacs, available from summer 2005 at $30,000, soothes you with music, images of nature and a mechanical massage. Matsushita representative Takahiro Heiuchi has said: 'Nobody who's come in here for 30 minutes hasn't fallen asleep.' Back in the real countryside, Claire Forrest, officer for the Chilterns Conservation Board, is researching the nature of tranquillity. Writing in the *Bucks Free Press,* she asks whether increasing awareness of technology in rural areas, from light pollution to mobile-phone masts, challenges the perception of, and/or our experience of, tranquillity.

Below
Zbigniew Oksiuta's Cosmic Bubble, a polymeric
form free-shaped in zero gravity.

Remote Sense

As part of British Telecom's remote-monitoring business (Redcare), the company has launched Vend Online. Working with Cadbury Trebor Bassett (CTB) and Sielaff (vending-machine suppliers), it has developed telemetry-enabled vending machines that can provide operators with 24-hour remote access to sales figures, and prevent what BT describes as an 'out-of-stock situation'. Using Vend Online, alerts can be sent as SMS text messages to representatives. According to Chris Morgan, customer relations director of CTB: 'This technology has demonstrated double-digit sales increases when tested. A vending operator can anticipate what a customer wants and when they want it, and machine downtime is minimal.' Vend Online is one of a range of Redcare products, which also includes vehicle tracking, remote domestic security and Coldcall, which monitors food storage temperatures via an on-site data logger and alerts kitchen staff via SMS when food safety is at risk. Meanwhile, more remote sensing is to be trailed in Kerala, India, as reported in the *Hindustan Times*. Theft-prone sandalwood trees are being electronically tagged and tracked via one of India's 26 satellites (figures from *The Satellite Encyclopaedia*). This is part of India's enlightened space race, which saw the launch in 2004 of EDUSAT, the country's first dedicated education satellite, which is broadcasting programmes in local languages to 1,000 schools across India, a figure that

> Theft-prone sandalwood trees are being electronically tagged and tracked via one of India's 26 satellites (figures from *The Satellite Encyclopaedia*). This is part of India's enlightened space race, which saw the launch in 2004 of EDUSAT, the country's first dedicated education satellite, which is broadcasting programmes in local languages to 1,000 schools across India, a figure that will eventually rise to 10,000 schools within the next three years.

will eventually rise to 10,000 schools within the next three years. Other launches being planned by the Indian Space Research Organisation (ISRO) are for AGRISAT and HEALTHSAT, providing agricultural data and telemedicine services respectively. Buckminster Fuller would be proud.

Good Enough To Eat

Recent Archilab exhibitor Zbigniew Oksiuta argues that most of what is generally described as organic, fluid or dynamic architecture is no such thing, and its relationship with biology is limited or analogical only. His Spatium Gelatum (frozen space) project is designed to explore new architectures and their relationship with biological sciences. 'The space of the Spatium Gelatum will possess different tastes, smells and be edible.' To create spatial forms, Oksiuta examines the concept of isopycnic systems (neutral buoyancy), the technology of lava lamps, Frei Otto's work on the Pneu as one of nature's basic construction forms, and what he calls Lane Kluski technology or, translated from Polish, 'the cooking of poached dumplings'. Initial prototypes have been fabricated with the biological polymer by-product gelatine. At the consumption end of the market, there has been renewed interest in the antimicrobial properties of silver. These properties were used by the conciliatory conqueror Cyrus the Great 2,500 years ago in his armies' silver-lined water flasks, and in the silver coin said to be placed in the water bottles of Roman soldiers. The silver service indeed functioned not only as a reflection of societal status, but also had a more practical property in electrocuting bugs. At a recent conference in London, looking at the future of nanotechnology and its applications, silver-coated nanofibres were featured in medical textiles (from bed linen to bandages) and in clothing, eliminating microbes and smell. Colloidal silver products were also demonstrated as an admixture in paints, tile grouting and fine coatings for food storage, and air and water filters. Δ+

McLean's Nuggets is an ongoing technical series inspired by Will McLean's and Samantha Hardingham's enthusiasm for back issues of Δ, as explicitly explored in Hardingham's Δ issue *The 1970s Is Here and Now* (March/April 2005).

Will McLean is joint coordinator (with Pete Silver) of technical studies in the Department of Architecture at the University of Westminster, and is currently working on designs for new primary schools with artist Bruce McLean and North Ayrshire Council.

Below
Let's Eat, Melbourne, Australia
Designer: Landini & Associates
Chefs cook food in open-plan kitchens for customers to eat in or take away.

Eye to Heart to Mouth

Designing food shops is about so much more than creating a visually appealing environment. As **Jane Peyton** explains, in order to whet appetites you have to be sure not only of triggering shoppers' senses, but also of subliminally keying in to their emotions.

Below
Harris Teeter supermarket, Charlotte, North Carolina, US
Designer: Little Diversified Architectural Consulting
The choice of colour for this dramatic entrance has a
psychological and physical effect on shoppers.

'People shop with their senses. Taste this, squeeze that, fill your lungs with the aroma and feast with your eyes.' Mark Landini of Landini & Associates made this comment whilst I was talking to him as part of my research for the Interior Angles book *Fabulous Food Shops*. When another retail designer, Gabriel Murray, mentioned something similar, that 'People eat with their eyes,' it made me realise how intrinsic psychology is to shopping. Like most people, I was already aware of the aroma of freshly baked bread, a supermarket trick that makes people feel so hungry that they pile extra goods into their trolleys, but I wondered whether designers of food shops also took other psychological factors into account.

Shopping for food is more than just filling up a basket – subconsciously, it is a right-brain left-brain experience where practicalities meet an emotional response. By understanding psychology, designers can create shops that exploit customers' motivations; for example, budget, convenience, desire, indulgence, largesse, lifestyle, aspirations, conscience, sense of adventure, playfulness, choice of merchandise, presentation, hygiene and nostalgia. I was surprised to learn that the majority of these motivators can be satisfied by the use of key visual anchors in a design, giving clues to the style, content and attitude of the store. When shoppers spot these anchors, they feel assured that they have come to the right place and that their needs will be met. Does the deli have a stainless-steel counter (denotes cleanliness and quality)? Is there floor-to-ceiling shelving full of merchandise (suggests food authority and an adventure of discovery)?

What the customer initially perceives will determine whether he or she stays and shops or leaves without purchasing anything. For instance, the shopper in a hurry and on a budget walks into a supermarket and sees lines of aisles, multiple checkouts, simple navigational signage and a good choice of merchandise for a one-stop shop. What the individual senses by the design is that he or she can do his or her shopping quickly and cheaply. Exit a satisfied customer. Whereas the person planning a special dinner party visits a local gourmet food hall and finds organic produce in abundance spilling out of wooden display units (food presented in wood is perceived as being fresh and natural); the shop's lighting is as near to daylight as possible so that the colours of the fruit and vegetables are true; and walls are lined with oak shelves of hard-to-find goodies imported from Italy and France. This shopper enjoys the adventure of choosing something wonderful to serve for his or her guests and has a thoroughly pleasurable shopping experience. And whether these two consumers realise it or not, the design of the shop has contributed to the positive shopping events.

One of the most effective and simple ways of influencing a food shopper is by the use of colour. Take, for example, the supermarket Harris Teeter in Charlotte, North Carolina, designed by Little Diversified Architectural Consulting. It boasts a dramatic red passageway that leads from the car park to the shop floor. The designer's goal was to create a compression zone as a prelude to entering the store, preparing

One of the most effective and simple ways of influencing a food shopper is by the use of colour. Take, for example, the supermarket Harris Teeter in Charlotte, North Carolina, designed by Little Diversified Architectural Consulting. It boasts a dramatic red passageway that leads from the car park to the shop floor. The designer's goal was to create a compression zone as a prelude to entering the store, preparing customers for a theatrical shopping experience.

Appealing to a customer's aspirations by choice of design language is a winner. A smart and stylish concept that merits coverage in fashionable media outlets will attract shoppers who want to see and be seen. It is important to them that they are considered up-to-the-minute. Landini & Associates recognised that lifestyle and how people perceive themselves are important considerations when designing a food shop.

customers for a theatrical shopping experience. Psychologically, the colour red is very powerful – it is attention-grabbing, friendly, lively and stimulating, and raises the pulse rate. In the seconds it takes a person to walk along the corridor, he or she will have undergone a subtle mood change, and will be charged up for shopping.

Green, by contrast, denotes harmony, peace, refreshment and environmental awareness. On a primal level, we are reassured when our surroundings are green – it means water must be present, so there is little chance of famine. It suggests plenty and harvest, so the use of this colour in greengrocers and natural food shops is a sensible choice. Shoppers will perceive freshness, abundance and nature in the merchandise, and place their trust in it.

Customer loyalty can be earned when shoppers feel that the owner respects them and their opinion. When Sainsbury's commissioned 20|20 to develop a new store in Hazel Grove, Cheshire, the design consultancy asked customers what they wanted from a supermarket. Several of these suggestions were incorporated into the final design, including a children's play zone that contains exhibits from the Science Museum, and a comfy sit-down area with an Internet café in which people can wait whilst mum does the shopping. With 20|20's positive response to customers' ideas, shoppers may feel it is 'their' store. Another example which involved the clientele was when Little Diversified Architectural Consulting included locals in several aspects of the design process of a new branch of Harris Teeter in Nashville. Customers got the store they truly wanted and now have an emotional investment in it, so are loyal to this shop and the company as a whole.

Appealing to a customer's aspirations by choice of design language is a winner. A smart and stylish concept that merits coverage in fashionable media outlets will attract shoppers who want to see and be seen. It is important to them that they are considered up-to-the-minute. Landini & Associates recognised that lifestyle and how people perceive themselves are important considerations when designing a food shop. Their seminal 1998 project, Let's Eat, in Melbourne, presented shoppers with an ultramodern store and theatrical shopping experience. It included open kitchens where chefs prepared food from the shop floor to be eaten at serve-over counters or taken home, as well as tear-off recipe sheets and cooking hints dotted around the store, and a licensed bar. And in 2002, Future Systems designed a unique and singular food hall for Selfridges in Manchester's Exchange Square. It is chic, curvaceous and sexy, and by incorporating several sit-up food and drinks counters, became a very smart place to people-watch as customers ate oysters and drank champagne before or after shopping for an undeniably superb selection of foodstuff.

So now that I understand a little about psychology as a useful design tool, I play a game with myself to see what mental buttons are being pushed when I'm out food shopping. It is very disappointing if I come away with a no-score draw. **△+**

Note
Let's Eat, in Melbourne, now trades under the name The Essential Ingredient, and whilst the design is little altered, the retailing concept has changed significantly.

Jane Peyton is a London-based writer. Her recent book *Fabulous Food Shops* (see www.fabulousfoodshops.com) is her third for Wiley-Academy, and follows *Looking Up in London* (www.lookingupinlondon.com) and *Looking Up in Edinburgh* (www.lookingupinedinburgh.com). She is currently working on another title in the Interior Angles series, which focuses on the world's most visually appealing pubs.

Below
Toying with nature: a house outside Sydney.

Walters and Cohen

Jeremy Melvin examines the work of a London-based, South-African-born partnership, whose first commission was for an art gallery in Durban. He discovers how Cindy Walters and Michál Cohen are now able, in the UK, to put to good use the analytical skills wrought out of an atmosphere of political instability and uncertainty in their home country – a background that has enabled them to work fruitfully with the British policy-making establishment of government and the old-school establishment at Bedales.

Top
Site plan of the art gallery in Durban, showing how the
design maximises exterior space.

Bottom
Placing the new gallery in a long, thin shape on one side
of the site maximised an outdoor public precinct.

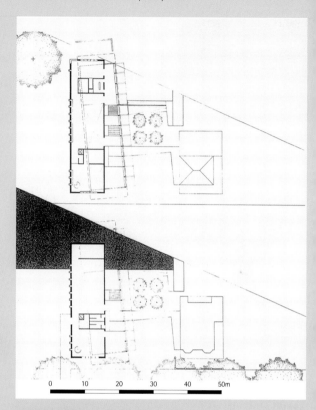

Young architectural firms might expect to have a varied
workload, as the serendipity of early commissions takes time
to harden into specific skills and reputations. More than a
decade after its foundation, at one level Walters and Cohen's
remains as varied as any, ranging from private houses and art
galleries, through luxurious health clubs and exclusive private
schools to primary schools in deprived cities. But somewhere
beneath the superficial variance of building types and client
organisations there is a deeper level of consistency, which
seems to hinge around an interest in the relationship between
public space, public buildings and the services they provide.
Operating largely in the territory that opened up in Britain
with the advent of the National Lottery and the reappraisal
of what public buildings might be and should do that followed,
Walters and Cohen has been able to transcend the old Welfare
Statist straitjackets that placed freestanding unifunctional
buildings in an ill-defined public realm. Instead, their buildings
always engage with a site and its surroundings, as the first step
to suggesting that there may be some positive engagement
between a building, what goes on inside it and wider social
patterns. In short, their work starts to indicate how
architecture and public life might forge a new relationship for
the 21st century.

As the British government wrestles with reform of public
services, this may seem a peculiarly British story. Certainly,
several of Walters and Cohen's more important commissions
stem directly from the policy initiatives that flow from
governmental conundrums. But, ironically, Cindy Walters
and Michál Cohen both grew up and studied in South Africa.
As students in Durban during the 1980s, they saw the
consequences of a political regime that systematically withheld
both the possibility of public life and the benefits of social
services to the majority of its population. Cindy Walters is
reluctant to extrapolate too much from the experience, but does
accept that when she came to London as a young graduate at
the end of the 1980s, she could not take anything for granted.
Locals might fall into easy patterns they know; as an outsider
everything demands examination. The firm's first commission,
a competition win in 1994, the year of Nelson Mandela's
ascent to the presidency, was for an art gallery in Durban.

Not surprisingly, given the extraordinary conditions arising
from the perversions of apartheid and the euphoria that
followed its demise, it would be easy to dismiss art and
architecture as irrelevant. But Mandela chose the
symbolically important setting of Herbert Baker's colonial-
era Union Buildings in Pretoria for his inauguration, and
that event inspired whole genres of celebratory artistic
representations. Among the many challenges facing
architecture was the need to suggest the possibility of a
public life taking place in a public realm enriched by public
institutions – all of which apartheid had systematically
denied to, or withheld from, the majority of the population.
Despite the Durban gallery's small size and limited budget,
all of these fell within its remit, with its varied programme
of exhibitions and all-night parties.

Top
The competition design for the Wakefield Gallery explored the
possibility of a public institution marking its civic presence.

Bottom left
The competition entry for a gallery in Woking interwove the
gallery with public space and the canal.

Bottom right
The Canary Wharf health club brings a coenobitic atmosphere
more commonly associated with Swiss spas.

In its design, particularly in the way it combines a simple and
clear constructional aesthetic with a wish to maximise public
space on the site by placing the building along one edge, and
in bringing both aesthetic and site plan into relation with the
programme, it contains the seeds of many of their subsequent
interests. The firm's entry for the Wakefield Art Gallery developed
the theme of how the civic and social role of an art gallery
might be celebrated, while another entry for an art gallery in
Woking developed, in its site planning, the relationship between
public space and the institution. Walters and Cohen proposed
putting the gallery itself on a thin strip of land adjacent to
a canal, with the café bridging over the water with views
in either direction and a public route alongside the canal.

South Africa may have exposed Walters and Cohen
to the extreme consequences of denying the possibility
of public life and the role architecture can play in it,
but Britain during the second half of the 1990s faced
diluted forms of similar issues. It was already apparent
that the particular entanglement between public
services and Modernist architecture that had
underpinned the British Welfare State had long
outlived its usefulness. Public commissions, ravaged
by governmental parsimony and practices like
compulsory competitive tendering, were almost
moribund, so architecture had retreated into the private
realm of luxury housing, restaurants, shops and
leisure facilities. One aspect of Walters and Cohen's
early commissions reflects these circumstances.
It included the almost inevitable rite of passage for
young architects, of domestic commissions. In them
they showed an ability to achieve refined and sensory
aesthetic effects which they developed in a series
of health clubs, culminating in one at Canary Wharf,
probably the most sensual architectural experience
outside Vals, in Switzerland.

But the late 1990s also saw the emergence of a
series of policy initiatives – more by stealth and
accident than any systematic programme – that
offered the possibility of a new public architecture.
During the dying days of the Conservative government
the National Lottery came on stream, but the Tories
also introduced the radical, but sensible, concept of

Top left
School for the Future:
plan.

Middle
School for the Future:
cross section.

Bottom
School for the Future:
long section.

Top right
School for the Future:
interior perspective.

encouraging different public-service providers to talk to each other, and even to go into partnership. With different twists the Labour government, which came to power in 1997, has continued many of these trends. And this has set the scene for another aspect of Walters and Cohen's early work: a series of Sure Start nurseries, a government-backed initiative intended to give children security and early education while their parents can prepare to, and ultimately, return to work.

In a rare coincidence, both clients and architects were struggling to find ways of using buildings to serve their headline programmes and also contribute some greater sense of public benefit. Even if the motivations were not closely related they did at least overlap, and with initiatives that stemmed from them Walters and Cohen were able to take their ideas to a new level.

A crucial element in this process was the Schools for the Future competition, run by the Department for Education and Skills in 2003. Entrants were invited to consider what the future of schools might be, with an open agenda. Walters and Cohen was one of 11 selected from 63, and along with four others was asked to look at primary schools. Another five concentrated on secondary schools, and the last considered an 'all-through' school. Working with environmental engineers Max Fordham LLP, structural engineers Adams Kara Taylor and quantity surveyors Davis Langdon LLP, Walters and Cohen speculated on the future of classrooms in the age of IT, the optimum orientation for best daylight and heating conditions, and how to

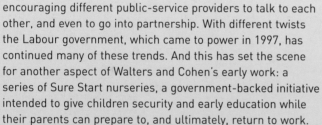

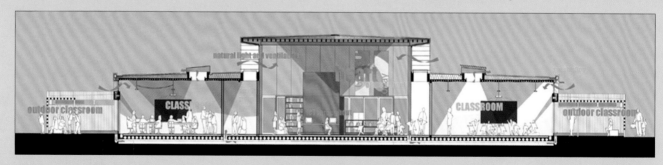

Bottom
School for the Future plan: form and function work together to organise the school's
activities and its precinct, and to bring interactive benefit to the surroundings.

Top right
Site model of Bedales: three new buildings run from the left. The
library is in the top-left corner and the theatre is centre right.

Middle
The three new Bedales buildings are placed in relation to each other
and existing buildings, to modulate immediate outside spaces.

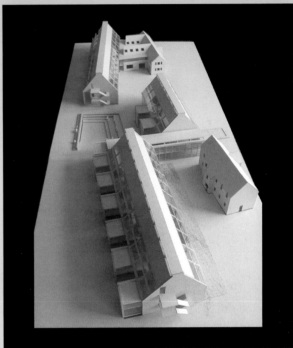

encourage a sense of interaction with the community without compromising security.

One effect was an almost total reconfiguration of the relationship of spaces to each other. They had quickly identified that areas like corridors and toilets were problematic, as they lacked ownership and clear purpose. But by recognising the potential of such spaces for 'incidental learning', and by concentrating them as much as possible in central, social areas, they turned drawback to advantage. By spreading learning throughout the building, the classroom loses its fetishistic status and becomes an organically integrated component of a machine for educating. If such an approach can be extended beyond the limitations of the building envelope, then a school can become less of a monument to 'authority', and more an integral part of everyday life.

Walters and Cohen's School for the Future was an opportunity to look at the sort of configurations that might work generically, such as the ideal orientation of a classroom for natural light and energy-conscious heating, and how classrooms might relate to shared and outdoor spaces. But the public face of the school was also crucial, and for this reason a forecourt became a vital element in the design. As further commissions flowed from this high-profile generic project, the firm began to harden the way these aims would work in practice. It became involved in schools in deprived areas of Stafford in the English Midlands, and Pontefract in Yorkshire, but most far-reaching of all is its participation in the Private Finance Initiative consortium bidding to build and maintain schools in Norwich.

Creating five new primary schools in place of 12, and extending a secondary school if the consortium is successful, will be, as Michál Cohen says, a test of their philosophy for schools. Some of the sites are too small to

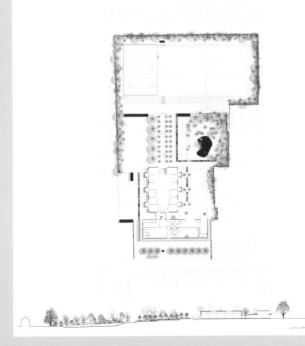

fit all the accommodation into a single storey, so they will have more than one level. Each is intended to be the centre of their immediate community and to offer more than education for local children. Social services and healthcare facilities may be incorporated into the design, creating a complex mix of uses but one which increases the sense of treating the design, including its precinct, as a piece of the public realm. With the private backers eager to obtain the highest possible intensity of use for any buildings they construct, this sort of interaction would not have been possible without this new mode of procurement. The challenge for architects is to find resolutions to the functional and aesthetic questions it poses.

There are even occasions, confirms Cindy Walters, when changes forced on to a generic model by practical circumstances lead to beneficial cross-fertilisation. As a private boarding school, Bedales has the sort of 24-hour life that educationalists in inner-city Norwich might envy, though with its 120-acre site and

121+

Top
Site plan for Bedales school, with the theatre to the left, the library towards the bottom and the house to the right.

Middle left
The environmental strategy at Bedales, worked out with Max Fordham LLP, maximised the advantages of orientation and the generic form of the buildings.

Middle right
The new Bedales buildings will create a protected, sunken courtyard.

Bottom
Bedales master plan.

KEY

1. Main arrival
2. Drop off/deliveries
3. **New green car park; cars screened by hedges**
4. New school entrance
5. New living space
6. New teaching garden
7. New teaching building
8. New reflective garden
9. Existing ICT building
10. **Existing geography building**
11. **New administration building**
12. New art court
13. New art, design and technology building
14. New gallery
15. Existing theatre
16. New theatre square
17. **New south-facing gardens**
18. **New brick path leading to the quad**
19. **Existing orchard with new trees**
20. Existing gymnasium
21. **Existing music building**
22. Existing Lupton Hall
23. **Existing memorial library**
24. Existing Steephurst

New built

— Demolition
— **Extension of proposed works**

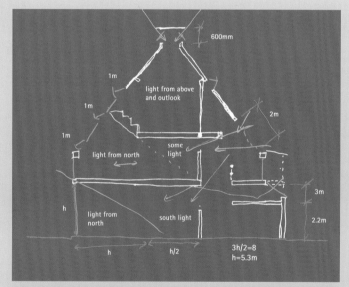

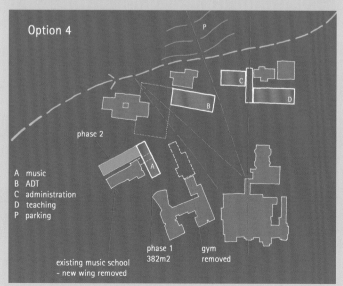

Option 4

A music
B ADT
C administration
D teaching
P parking

phase 2

phase 1
382m2

gym
removed

existing music school
- new wing removed

well-heeled parents and alumni it hardly faces the same spatial and financial conditions. Even so, the new classroom blocks rise to three storeys. This is partly to respect the large volumes of several distinguished buildings: a large 17th-century farmhouse, a recent theatre by Feilden Clegg and, in particular, the Arts and Crafts library by Ernest Gimson and Sidney Barnsley. Based on a traditional barn, this magnificent space arranges the books in two-storey alcoves around a double-height central aisle, and the new teaching blocks pick up much from this configuration. Classrooms of varying sizes are clustered around central spines allowing views to different levels and to protected outdoor areas.

Such a negotiation between site and programme underlies all of Walters and Cohen's projects, and the iterative accumulation helps to lend consistency to their

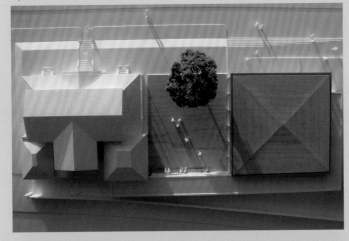

work. If these are two axes, their point of intersection occurs where designs create spaces that offer realistic possibilities for activities, and that fit as closely into local patterns of use as comfortably as the forms fit into their physical context. Making a public space outside the Durban gallery may well have been necessary to give the institution an acceptable public presence, but the same formal principles arise in more recent projects for the Royal Botanical Gardens at Kew and its rural outpost at Wakehurst Place. The Gallery of Botanical Art is technically an extension to a Victorian house in the original gardens; it consciously forms an open space between old and new, a space that becomes significant in its own right, though its arrangement reflects the configuration of the Temperate House with which it almost forms an axis.

As a freestanding building required to minimise visual impact in the landscape, the visitors' centre at Wakehurst Place necessarily has a different relationship to its context. On a restricted budget it became at one level an exercise in economical construction; and the precise function of visitors' centres is notoriously difficult to define. Yet by taking a cue from the dual needs of visual discretion and economy, Walters and Cohen used slender steelwork and walls of glass and tropical hardwood, which British customs confiscate and pass on to Kew for educational purposes, to give the design a subtle discretion. This might reflect the building's minor status in relation to the park, but it also recalls the side of Modernism represented by the Case Study houses, which contrasts with the Kahnian vaults of the site's principal recent building, Stanton Williams' Millennium Seed Bank. Even though function, budget and setting determine that the building has a minor role, a sense of architecture's cultural potential still runs through it. It is these values that guide Walters and Cohen as they strive to reconnect the public realm with public services, institutions and architecture.

Cindy Walters

Walters and Cohen

Resumé

Founded 1994: grown to 17 staff.
Single office in north London

Michál Cohen

Current projects
Bedales secondary school, Hampshire
Art gallery, Kew Gardens
Primary school, Pontefract, West Yorkshire
Primary school, Rugeley, Staffordshire
Five primary schools, Norwich (PFI)
Children's Centre, Peckham, London
Children's Centre, Hackney, London
New restaurant, Wakehurst Place, West Sussex
(Royal Botanical Gardens rural site)

Completed projects
2004	Hollingdean Parent and Child Centre, Brighton
	Visitor centre, Wakehurst Place, West Sussex
2003	DfES exemplar school, non-site-specific
	Occupational health centre, Bank of England, London
	Private house, Sydney
	Nursery, Royal Docks, London
2002	Penthouses, Canary Wharf, London
	Private house, Crouch End, London
2001	Nursery, Southwark, London
	Spa, Canary Wharf, London
	Private house, Primrose Hill, London
2000	Offices, Stockley Park, Uxbridge
	Health club, Elstree
1999	Health club, Islington, London
	Nursery, Wandsworth, London
	Offices, Camden, London
	Private house, Fulham, London
1998	Private house, Tobago
	Nursery, Stockley Park, Uxbridge
	Offices, Kensington, London
1997	Health club, Wood Green, London
	Nursery, Bristol
1996	Art gallery, Durban, South Africa
	Health club, Chelsea, London
	Private house, Belsize Park, London
	Private house, Hampstead, London

Competitions
2004	Nottingham art gallery; runner-up
	Aldeburgh music campus, Snape Maltings; runner-up
	Art gallery, Wakefield; shortlisted
2003	Royal Botanic Gardens, Kew, Framework Agreement
	Whitechapel art gallery; shortlisted
	Bedales school; first place
	DfES exemplar school; first place
2002	Art gallery, Woking; runner-up
	Health centre, Bank of England; first place
	Hollingdean Parent and Child Centre; first place
	RIBA competition, housing, Hampshire; first place
2001	Finsbury Hub; runner-up
	Nursery, Sheffield; first place
	Nursery and community centre, Bloomsbury, London; shortlisted
	Rainbow community centre; first place
	Sports club, Wandsworth, London; first place
	RIBA competition: Sustainable school, RIBA; first place
2000	Nursery, Southwark, London; first place
	National Centre for Photography in Wales; first place
1999	Yehudi Menuhin School, new recital hall and music teaching facilities; first place
1997	Memorial chapel, Pangbourne; runner-up
1995	Art gallery, Durban; first place

Key staff
Cindy Walters, Partner
Born: Australia
Studied: University of Natal, South Africa
Foster and Partners 1988–94 working on
various projects including Carré d'Art in Nîmes
English National Opera,
redevelopment of London Coliseum
Walters and Cohen 1994–

Michál Cohen, Partner
Born: South Africa
Studied: University of Natal, South Africa
Geraghty Little McCaffrey 1988–91 (South Africa);
Koski Solomon and Ruthven (London) 1991–4;
Walters and Cohen 1994–

Giovanni Bonfanti, Associate
Born: Milan, Italy
Studied: University of Venice, Italy
Worked in Venice, Milan, London
Walters and Cohen 1997–;
Associate 2001–

Elaine Henderson, Associate
Born: Ireland
Diploma in Architectural Technology 1993
Graduated Architectural Association, London 1999
Walters and Cohen, 1996–;
Associate 2001–

Bozana Komljenovich, Associate
Born: Belgrade
Studied: Belgrade University and
South Bank University, London
Walters and Cohen 1998–;
Associate 2002–

Clients
Bank of England
Bedales school
Brighton and Hove City Council
Canary Riverside Plc
Charterhouse-in-Southwark
Department for Education and Skills
Ffotogallery
Guildhouse Group
Harbour Land Developments Ltd
Holmes Place Plc
Investec
Jigsaw Day Nurseries Plc
Joint Schools Property Unit (for Stafford LA)
KwaZulu Natal Society of Arts
London and Regional Properties
London Borough of Hackney
London Borough of Southwark
Ministry of Defence
Neath Port Talbot County Borough Council
NPS North East Ltd (for Wakefield LA)
Royal Botanic Gardens, Kew
Sorrell Foundation
Stockley Park Consortium
Swaythling Housing Association *D+*

Below
Visitors descend into the underground barrel cellar which features a concrete vaulted ceiling and an integrated entertainment zone for special tastings and dinners. The heat sink effect of the surrounding earth maintains the stable, cool and humid environment ideal for barrel ageing.

Jackson-Triggs

Niagara Estate Winery

Sean Stanwick looks at a contemporary winery designed by Kuwabara Payne McKenna Blumberg Architects (KPMB) in Ontario, Canada, for the same client as Frank Gehry's in Le Clos Jordanne.

Below
The gravity-feed system was also adapted as a metaphor for the
choreography of the winery tour. In the final act, visitors reascend into the
tasting gallery and retail shop to appreciate the product at first hand.

Ask any vintner about 'terroir' and they will gleefully illuminate how each and every grape is completely influenced by the soil from which it grows. Ask architects Kuwabara Payne McKenna Blumberg (KPMB) about the Jackson-Triggs Niagara Estate winery and you will likely get the same answer. In a place where wine is the hero, it is no accident that production, the architecture and the tour are cut from the same vine and bottled into a finely tuned, theatrical experience.

At the helm of the operation is the enigmatic Don Triggs, CEO of the Ontario-based Vincor International Inc, also the same client who brought Frank Gehry to Canada with his first freestanding building in Le Clos Jordanne. Vincor is North America's fourth-largest producer and marketer of wines
and wanted a building that would support the growth and the international reputation of Canadian-made products while simultaneously enhancing the agro-tourist experience for vine-o-philes embarking on the Niagara Wine Tour – an annual Ontario summer ritual.

Interestingly, for all their combined experience, neither Triggs nor KPMB had ever actually designed a new winery before. Several trips through the Napa Valley would prove invaluable as the team learned first-hand the techniques of the gravity-feed process. But, more importantly, the Napa trips made clear the benefits of marrying the science of 'wine making' with the art of 'wine marketing'.

Operating more like a carefully choreographed theatrical event, the Niagara Wine Tour is a wonderfully fluid experience that physically mimics the gravity-feed process itself. Hosted by the same person from start to finish, visitors literally flow along with the wine and follow the sequence from fruit and vine to bottling and sales with, of course, stops for tasting and reflection along the way. Although it's not formally part of the tour proper, the opening act begins in the meandering approach through several small vineyards. The official tour begins in the great hall, a mammoth cut through the whole of the building with enormous barn-like sliding doors that allow the winery to freely open itself to the panorama and the seasonal summer breezes blowing from the vineyards beyond. Here, sliding oak screens echo its agrarian roots and speak to the barrels lying in wait in the cellars below, while polished white marble tasting-counters provide a neutral backdrop against the vibrant colours of the wine displayed in

> Interestingly, for all their combined experience, neither Triggs nor KPMB had ever actually designed a new winery before. Several trips through the Napa Valley would prove invaluable as the team learned first-hand the techniques of the gravity-feed process. But, more importantly, the Napa trips made clear the benefits of marrying the science of 'wine making' with the art of 'wine marketing'.

recessed wall niches.

Once greeted, visitors ascend an exterior ramp to penetrate
the space of the wooden rafters of the fermentation room,
where a series of suspended catwalks provide aerial viewing of
the crushing vats and stainless-steel fermentation tanks below.
From here, visitors pass and wedge precariously between the
massive tanks and descend directly to the cellar; a dimly lit
concrete barrel-vault with its oak charges lying in wait. But, as
expected, the wine takes centre stage and for all its modern
cadence and polished earthy tones, time stands still in the
warm presence of the rows of ageing barrels.

From the silence of the cellar, visitors reascend to the
tasting gallery and, in the final act, are treated to a variety
of wines, a brief lesson on appropriate glass selection and,
hopefully, a lasting appreciation of viticulture and the wine-
making environment. As an encore, the winery also supports
intensive hospitality events such as VIP tastings for two, eight-
course dinners for a hundred guests and, recently, live
performances in an outdoor amphitheatre. In the cellar there
is an entertainment zone for special events.

If it is indeed true that soil, climate and orientation impart
unique qualities to each individual grape, then the same can
easily be said of the building itself. Sited to maximise the
arable vineyard area and to benefit from the dense greenery
on the Two Mile Creek edge, the winery is typically KPMB who,
like a good merlot, rely on a refined and subtle blend of local
ingredients to warm the palate. Far removed from the typical
European chateau, it has more in common with its rural
ancestors. Set upon a plinth of natural stone, and with exposed
beams of fir, spears of aluminium and random shafts of light,
on seeing it one cannot help but feel like one has stumbled
upon a country barn long-forgotten.

Through the new winery, sales, production and brand
perception have all enjoyed tremendous growth and,
most importantly, Triggs has raised the status of the
bar by providing a comprehensive wine experience for
wine lovers, tourists and architectural aficionados alike.
Named 'Best Canadian Winery' at Vinitaly 2002 in
Verona, the portfolio currently consists of VQA table
wines, sparkling and ice wines, carrying either the
black 'Proprietors' Reserve' label or the rarer gold
'Grand Reserve', reserved for limited-edition wines
available exclusively at the winery. Δ+

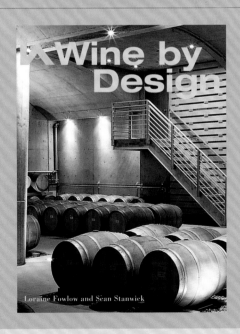

Sean Stanwick is co-author with Loraine Fowlow of *Wine by Design: The
Space of Wine* in the Interior Angles series to be published by Wiley-Academy
in the autumn of 2005.

Subscribe Now

As an influential and prestigious architectural publication, *Architectural Design* has an almost unrivalled reputation worldwide. Published bimonthly, it successfully combines the currency and topicality of a newsstand journal with the editorial rigour and design qualities of a book. Consistently at the forefront of cultural thought and design since the 1960s, it has time and again proved provocative and inspirational – inspiring theoretical, creative and technological advances. Prominent in the 1980s for the part it played in Postmodernism and then in Deconstruction, ⚠ has recently taken a pioneering role in the technological revolution of the 1990s. With groundbreaking titles dealing with cyberspace and hypersurface architecture, it has pursued the conceptual and critical implications of high-end computer software and virtual realities. ⚠

⚠ Architectural Design

SUBSCRIPTION RATES 2005

Institutional Rate (Print only or Online only): UK£175/US$290
Institutional Rate (Combined Print and Online): UK£193/US£320
Personal Rate (Print only): UK£99/US$155
Discount Student* Rate (Print only): UK£70/US$110

*Proof of studentship will be required when placing an order. Prices reflect rates for a 2005 subscription and are subject to change without notice.

TO SUBSCRIBE

Phone your credit card order:
+44 (0)1243 843 828

Fax your credit card order to:
+44 (0)1243 770 432

Email your credit card order to:
cs-journals@wiley.co.uk

Post your credit card or cheque order to:
John Wiley & Sons Ltd.
Journals Administration Department
1 Oldlands Way
Bognor Regis
West Sussex PO22 9SA
UK

Please include your postal delivery address with your order.

All ⚠ volumes are available individual. To place an order please write to:
John Wiley & Sons Ltd
Customer Services
1 Oldlands Way
Bognor Regis
West Sussex PO22 9SA

Please quote the ISBN number of the issue(s) you are ordering.

⚠ is available to purchase on both a subscription basis and as individual volumes

---

○ I wish to subscribe to ⚠ *Architectural Design* at the **Institutional rate of (Print only or Online only** *(delete as applicable)* **£175/US$290.**

○ I wish to subscribe to ⚠ *Architectural Design* at the **Institutional rate of (Combined Print and Online) £193/US$320.**

○ I wish to subscribe to ⚠ *Architectural Design* at the **Personal rate of £99/US$155.**

○ I wish to subscribe to ⚠ *Architectural Design* at the **Student rate of £70/US$110.**

○ ⚠ *Architectural Design* is available to individuals on either a calendar year or rolling annual basis; Institutional subscriptions are only available on a calendar year basis. Tick this box if you would like your Personal or Student subscription on a rolling annual basis.

Payment enclosed by Cheque/Money order/Drafts.

Value/Currency £/US$ ▢

○ Please charge £/US$ ▢ to my credit card.
Account number:

▢▢▢▢▢▢▢▢▢▢▢▢▢▢▢▢▢▢

Expiry date:

▢▢▢▢▢▢

Card: Visa/Amex/Mastercard/Eurocard *(delete as applicable)*

Cardholder's signature ▢
Cardholder's name ▢
Address ▢
▢
▢ Post/Zip Code ▢

Recipient's name ▢
Address ▢
▢
▢ Post/Zip Code ▢

I would like to buy the following issues at £22.50 each:

○ ⚠ 175 *Food + The City*, Karen A Franck
○ ⚠ 174 *The 1970s Is Here and Now*, Samantha Hardingham
○ ⚠ 173 *4dspace: Interactive Architecture*, Lucy Bullivant
○ ⚠ 172 *Islam + Architecture*, Sabiha Foster
○ ⚠ 171 *Back To School*, Michael Chadwick
○ ⚠ 170 *The Challenge of Suburbia*, Ilka + Andreas Ruby
○ ⚠ 169 *Emergence*, Michael Hensel, Achim Menges + Michael Weinstock
○ ⚠ 168 *Extreme Sites*, Deborah Gans + Claire Weisz
○ ⚠ 167 *Property Development*, David Sokol
○ ⚠ 166 *Club Culture*, Eleanor Curtis
○ ⚠ 165 *Urban Flashes Asia*, Nicholas Boyarsky + Peter Lang
○ ⚠ 164 *Home Front: New Developments in Housing*, Lucy Bullivant
○ ⚠ 163 *Art + Architecture*, Ivan Margolius
○ ⚠ 162 *Surface Consciousness*, Mark Taylor
○ ⚠ 161 *Off the Radar*, Brian Carter + Annette LeCuyer
○ ⚠ 160 *Food + Architecture*, Karen A Franck
○ ⚠ 159 *Versioning in Architecture*, SHoP
○ ⚠ 158 *Furniture + Architecture*, Edwin Heathcote
○ ⚠ 157 *Reflexive Architecture*, Neil Spiller
○ ⚠ 156 *Poetics in Architecture*, Leon van Schaik
○ ⚠ 155 *Contemporary Techniques in Architecture*, Ali Rahim
○ ⚠ 154 *Fame and Architecture*, J. Chance and T. Schmiedeknecht
○ ⚠ 153 *Looking Back in Envy*, Jan Kaplicky
○ ⚠ 152 *Green Architecture*, Brian Edwards
○ ⚠ 151 *New Babylonians*, Iain Borden + Sandy McCreery
○ ⚠ 150 *Architecture + Animation*, Bob Fear